Eating and shopping in France

PAM BOURGEOIS

KOLIBRI

Acknowledgements

My thanks are due to Kari Masson as Managing Editor for her enthusiasm, encouragement and her excellent organisational and editing skills. She was an invaluable aid in getting everything into shape. I am particularly grateful for her support and belief in the project from the beginning.

Stephanie Hinderer as Artistic Director did a remarkable job on the cover and the overall style of the book. She has a great eye for detail, is extremely creative and made many constructive comments.

I would like to thank Christine Comte for her very professional approach to the book's layout and page design and for her unending patience. She brought great enthusiasm to the project as well as her considerable experience as a graphic designer.

My thanks, too, to Garth Lombard of Largemouth Frog Productions for his work on the audio recording and musical introduction and to the talented photographers who contributed to the visual appeal of this book.

I am also indebted to Erin Tremouilhac for her help in checking the facts and to Alison Tetlow and Jean-Marie Bel who read the draft copy and made thoughtful comments.

Series Editor: Pam Bourgeois
Managing Editor: Kari Masson
Artistic Director: Stephanie Hinderer
Graphic Designer: Christine Comte

Contents

Foreword   *6*

Part 1. **EATING OUT**   *7*

Un café   *8*
Une brasserie   *15*
Un restaurant   *22*
Une crêperie, un bouchon...   *29*

Part 2. **TRADITIONAL FOOD SHOPS**   *37*

Une boulangerie   *38*
Une pâtisserie chocolaterie   *45*
Une fromagerie   *52*
Une charcuterie traiteur   *59*

Part 3. **NOT TO BE MISSED**   *67*

Le marché   *68*
Un caveau   *75*
Les spécialités régionales   *82*
Le shopping à Paris   *89*

Foreword

My many years spent abroad as a French expatriate have taught me a thing or two. Firstly, learning about a new country, its culture, language and history is inseparable from experiencing its food, both regional and national. Secondly, this advice is never truer than for France, my home country, which boasts such an undeniable culture of culinary panache!

"Dis-moi ce que tu manges, je te dirai ce que tu es," [Tell me what you eat and I will tell you what you are] wrote Anthelme Brillat-Savarin, a French judge, doctor, politician and... gourmand in 1826 in PHYSIOLOGIE DU GOÛT, still considered a bible of gastronomy. It was no surprise when, in 2010, UNESCO added "the gastronomic meal of the French" to the intangible cultural heritage lists.

With simple, clear and down-to-earth tips, this practical guide will help you navigate through the richness of French culinary tradition and the variety of food and drinks that are quintessentially French. It will considerably enhance your understanding and your enjoyment of the social rituals of dining out in France, from the marrying of food with wine to the fixed structure of meals, the rich flavors of the terroir and the subtle manner in which you can trick your waiter into giving you the table you want, yes, that one by the window!

Preparing for a trip to France can be done in so many ways: studying French history, the political system, the economy (weeks of arduous reading), or by learning the language (years of study). This guide offers a crisp, well-written and amusing alternative which guarantees immediate gratification: eating your way through Parisian and regional foods as well as shopping for gifts and partaking in the traditional market scene, where French farmers proudly display their artisan cheeses and their freshly picked produce.

With a large sampling of useful French sentences, historical anecdotes, drôle French sayings and intelligent insights, *Eating and Shopping in France* is a welcome passport to the French lifestyle. Embark on a new way to enjoy France! Love it, love its food!

Danièle Thomas Easton
Former Honorary Consul of France in Philadelphia and Wilmington
Chevalier de la Légion d'Honneur (2007)
CEO of France-Philadelphie, consultancy for Franco-American companies and cultural projects

Part 1

EATING OUT

Un café

WHAT TO EXPECT

Sitting in the sun on the terrace of a French *café* with a cup of coffee is an enjoyable moment in every visitor's experience of France. For many French people, going to a *café* is simply part of their daily life.

No time for breakfast? A quick coffee and maybe a croissant at the bar of a local *café* is an easy alternative. For those who need something a little stronger to get them going, it is never too early for *un petit rouge* or *un petit blanc*, a glass of red or white wine. Mid-morning, a retired person may sit down and enjoy a coffee while reading the newspaper, or a student will settle at a corner table to study. At lunch, it's time for all the people cooped up in offices to have a snack or a salad while soaking up the sunshine on the *café*'s terrace. In the early evening, a *café* is the place for an *apéritif* before going home or for a meal at a restaurant, or simply for enjoying a warm summer's evening.

FOR MANY FRENCH PEOPLE, GOING TO A *CAFÉ* IS SIMPLY PART OF THEIR DAILY LIFE.

CULTURAL TIPS

In many towns, *cafés* without terraces are allowed to set up a few tables outside just for the summer months, creating small terraces even when there is very little space. A *café* without a terrace in the summer has a hard time competing. In the winter months, *cafés* with large, permanent terraces continue to attract clients by installing overhead heaters.

You can no longer smoke inside French *cafés*, but smoking is permitted on outside terraces.

Un café

The village *café*, so frequently a setting in films depicting French rural life, is still the place where the locals will meet up on market day or stop by to exchange gossip. If you join them, you may have the chance to watch a nearby game of *boules*, or you can just sit back and listen and try to understand the other customers' accents.

With the exception of some of the larger *cafés*, notably in Paris, the waiter may be dressed quite casually, but he or she will still be professional and will note when new customers arrive and are waiting to order. The waiter will wipe the table to remove any traces left by the previous customer and take your order and repeat it back to you. There won't be much conversation as there is no time to be wasted. While some customers may want to sit and relax, others will need to be quickly on their way.

◀) KEYWORDS

le comptoir	bar
la terrasse	terrace, outside
à l'ombre	in the shade
au soleil	in the sun
un grand crème	coffee with milk
un chocolat chaud	hot chocolate
un thé nature	tea without milk
une tisane	herbal tea
un express	espresso
un demi	half a pint of beer
un jus de fruit	fruit juice
une grenadine	grenadine syrup and lemonade
un coca	Coca-Cola
un Schweppes	tonic water
un croque-monsieur	toasted ham and cheese sandwich
une salade	salad
une glace	ice-cream
un parfum	flavour
une paille	straw
l'addition	bill

Un café

CULTURAL TIPS

It used to be customary to leave a small tip. Since the introduction of the euro, with higher-value coins, this has become less common. But you can leave any small change you receive when you pay.

In some *cafés*, if you drink your coffee at the bar, it will cost you a little less than drinking it while seated on the terrace. The prices of all drinks are listed near the bar, as this is a legal requirement.

Cafés will also display their license, which allows them to sell alcoholic drinks, together with a notice saying they cannot serve alcohol to minors.

Typical soft drinks are *un citron pressé*, freshly-squeezed lemon juice, or *un diabolo-menthe*, a mint syrup mixed with lemonade. In summer months, particularly in the south of France, a common *apéritif* will be *un pastis*, an aniseed-based alcohol to which water is added.

If you eat a snack and want to pay by credit card, you will often need to pay at the bar.

Some *cafés* will have a fixed minimum amount before you can pay by card.

Your drinks will be brought on a traditional round tray along with a saucer with your bill. In some *cafés*, particularly in busy city centres, you will be expected to pay immediately and your waiter will make a tear in your bill to show that you have done so. Otherwise, the waiter will leave you to pay when you are ready, and if you don't need change, you can simply leave the amount on the saucer when you go.

No one will be hurrying you. Whiling away a couple of hours, watching life go by, is as much appreciated by the French as by any visitor.

THE VILLAGE *CAFÉ* IS STILL THE PLACE WHERE THE LOCALS WILL MEET UP ON MARKET DAY OR STOP BY TO EXCHANGE GOSSIP.

🔊 IDIOMS

— *Le café du coin* is the local café.
— *Le jus* is slang for coffee.
— *Ça ne va pas t'arriver servi sur un plateau* means you are not going to get it handed to you on a plate.
— *Raconter des salades* means to tell stories.
— *L'additon est salée* means that the bill is steep.

Un café

HISTORY AND TRADITIONS

The local *café*, sometimes known as *un bar, un bistrot, un estaminet* or *un troquet*, depending on its style or the region of France, is the place where people go to discuss and debate. This has been the case since the 17th century.

Cafés were first established in France by traders who had seen similar establishments in Turkey and the Middle East. The earliest *cafés* were in Marseille around 1650, and shortly afterward in Lyon. It was not until 1672 that they appeared in Paris. They were unsavoury places and not well-frequented. Coffee was, however, beginning to become popular with the upper classes, who were the only ones able to afford it, and in 1686, Le Procope, a well-decorated *café* serving coffee, opened. It attracted writers such as Voltaire, Diderot and Rousseau. The tradition of the *café littéraire* had been created.

Le Procope and other similar establishments were places where ideas were discussed and information was exchanged. In the 18th century, not only French philosophers but also American political figures such as Benjamin Franklin and Thomas Jefferson were frequent visitors.

By the end of the century, there were more than 3,000 *cafés* in Paris, and districts such as Saint-Germain-les-Prés and Montmartre became famous for their *cafés* with zinc-covered bars.

In the 20th century, *cafés* in France, unlike their coffee shop equivalents in other countries where hot drinks and pastries are served, remain places where alcohol is also served and in some cases where cigarettes are sold, too. Despite their decreasing numbers, their vast diversity ranging from historical meeting places to local bars or modern hip *cafés* means they are still very much a part of French life.

🔊 USEFUL PHRASES

– Je préfère une table au soleil.
I prefer a table in the sun.
– Je peux prendre cette table ?
Can I take this table?
– Je prendrai un express avec un croissant, s'il vous plaît.
I'll have an espresso and a croissant, please.
– Un chocolat chaud et un thé citron, s'il vous plaît.
A hot chocolate and a tea with lemon, please.
– Un déca, s'il vous plaît.
A decaf coffee, please.
– C'est possible de manger quelque chose ?
Is it possible to have something to eat?
– Qu'est-ce que vous avez à manger ?
What do you have to eat?
– Deux boules de glace, s'il vous plaît.
Two scoops of ice-cream, please.
– Je vous dois combien ?
What do I owe you?
– Je peux payer par carte ?
Can I pay with a credit card?

Un café

CULTURAL TIPS

When ordering a coffee in France, many people will also order a glass of water. Sometimes this will be brought to you without you requesting it. The same is true if you order ice-cream.

Cafés usually open very early, around seven o'clock, for people on their way to work. They will remain open all day and close at ten or eleven in the evening.

Cafés may serve snacks or meals at lunchtime but not normally in the evening. Some *cafés* will only have a choice of sandwiches. A common snack is *un croque-monsieur*, a toasted ham and cheese sandwich. The typical meal is *un steak frites*, steak and chips. If you're travelling in France, make sure you don't stop for lunch too late. After two o'clock, most *cafés* in small towns and villages will no longer serve food.

🔊 LANGUAGE TIPS

If you go into a *café* around lunchtime, the waiter may ask you:
– *C'est pour manger ?*

This is so he can direct you to a table that is already set up for lunch if you are intending to eat. If you have chosen a table yourself, he may confirm whether you want to eat something or whether you just want a drink by asking:
– *Vous voulez voir le menu ?*
Do you want to see the menu?

He may also ask you whether you prefer a table in the sun or in the shade:
– *À l'ombre ou au soleil ?*

If your waiter gives you a choice of salads or ice-creams and you don't remember all of them, you can say:
– *Je ne me rappelle pas ce que vous avez dit en premier.*
I don't remember what you said first.
– *Vous pouvez répéter, s'il vous plaît ?*
Could you repeat that, please?

🔊 YOU WILL HEAR

– *Bonjour Monsieur/Madame.*
   Good morning/afternoon sir/madam.
– *Nous avons des salades composées et des sandwiches.*
   We have mixed salads and sandwiches.
– *Comme boisson ?*
   What would you like to drink?
– *Quel parfum pour la glace ?*
   What flavour of ice-cream do you want?
– *Je vous apporte ça tout de suite.*
   I'll bring that to you straightaway.
– *Vous pouvez régler maintenant, s'il vous plaît ?*
   Can you pay now, please?
– *Pour la carte c'est au bar, s'il vous plaît.*
   If you're paying by card, it's at the bar, please.

Un café

🔊 *Remember*

If you order a coffee, it will come in a small cup and be called *un express*. It can also be called *un petit noir*. You should ask for *un café bien serré* or *un café bien tassé* if you like your coffee really strong. If you prefer weaker coffee, ask for *un café allongé*. If you want your coffee with hot, frothy milk, you can ask for *un café crème*. An *express* with just a little milk is called *une noisette*. A decaffeinated coffee is *un décaféiné*, usually shortened to *un déca*.

If you order tea, you will be served with a cup or a teapot of hot water and a separate tea bag. Most French people prefer *un thé nature*. If you require milk, specify that you want cold milk or you will be given hot milk:
– Je peux avoir un peu de lait froid, s'il vous plaît ?

🔊 ADVANCED USEFUL PHRASES

– Cette table est disponible ?
Is this table free?
– C'est possible de se déplacer à l'intérieur ? Il fait trop froid dehors.
Can we move inside? It's too cold outside.
– On peut ouvrir le parasol ? Il fait vraiment chaud.
Can we open the parasol? It's really hot.
– Vous auriez une paille, s'il vous plaît, pour mon fils ?
Do you have a straw for my son, please?
– Vous avez un sandwich sans viande ?
Do you have any sandwiches without meat?
– On peut avoir un coca et deux verres, s'il vous plaît ?
Can we have a Coca-Cola and two glasses, please?
– Vous pouvez nous apporter une carafe d'eau et du pain, s'il vous plaît ?
Could you bring us some water and bread, please?
– Je peux vous régler maintenant, s'il vous plaît ?
Can I pay now, please?

 **LEARN MORE**

You can find more examples of ordering drinks in *Une brasserie*, p.15.

For further examples of paying by credit card, you can refer to *Un restaurant*, p.22.

Un café

Most famous

Le Procope is the oldest *café* in Paris and is the famed literary *café* established towards the end of the 17th century. It is located at 13, rue de l'Ancienne-Comédie. If you visit it today, you can still see numerous documents, a hat belonging to Napoleon and other symbols of the Enlightenment and the Revolution. The toilets are still labelled *Citoyens* and *Citoyennes* in true revolutionary style. Today, Le Procope is more a *brasserie* than a simple *café*.

Le Café de Flore opened in the Saint-Germain-des-Prés district in 1887. From 1930 on, it was the meeting place for many famous authors such as Queneau and Desnos, and later Jean-Paul Sartre and Simone de Beauvoir. This famous couple spent their days there and Sartre wrote, *"Cela peut vous sembler bizarre, mais nous étions au Flore chez nous"*. (It may seem odd, but when we were at the Flore we were at home.)

Le Deauville on Les Champs-Élysées is also among the many famed Parisian *cafés*.

Quiz

Fill in the blanks using the word bank below.
café, boule, dois, prendre, pressé, frites

A. Je peux _____ cette table ?

B. Un _____ bien tassé, s'il vous plaît.

C. Je voudrais un citron _____, s'il vous plaît.

D. Un demi et un steak _____, s'il vous plaît.

E. Une _____ de glace à la vanille, s'il vous plaît.

F. Je vous _____ combien ?

Answers: A. prendre, B. café, C. pressé, D. frites, E. boule, F. dois.

KEY POINTS

Cafés...

- are open throughout the day from about seven o'clock until at least ten in the evening.
- will sometimes serve snacks or light meals but usually only at breakfast or lunchtime.
- may have different prices for drinks at the bar compared to on the terrace.
- will allow you to smoke on the pavement terrace only.
- will have areas where people who are not eating but only having a drink can sit at lunchtime.

Une brasserie

Une brasserie

WHAT TO EXPECT

Silverware and glass clinking, waiters carrying large trays up over their shoulders and plates filled with *choucroute* and sausages: this is the scene reflected to you by the large mirrors lining the walls of a *brasserie*. If you want to have a truly French experience, eating lunch in a *brasserie* is a must. However, *brasseries* are not the place to have a quiet, intimate conversation over lunch as they are usually big and often noisy during peak hours.

Many French *brasseries* date from the late 19th or early 20th century and have dominant positions on the boulevards of a city centre. You can order simple, traditional dishes from waiters who pride themselves on efficient, professional service and admire what are often elaborately decorated dining rooms, many in Art Deco style. The bigger *brasseries* have high, ornate ceilings, brass handrails, banquette seating and lots of mirrors.

CULTURAL TIPS

Brasseries usually offer an unchanging printed menu with plenty of choices. At lunchtime, particularly, many *brasseries* have several combinations so that busy people can order just a starter, a main course and a coffee, or a main course and dessert. It is also possible just to order a single dish. Some business people may still order a full three-course meal with wine. The two-hour lunch break, which was common practice in France until quite recently is, however, now the exception rather than the rule and customers will expect even a full meal to be served quickly.

Sometimes the specialities of the day, or the choice of desserts, will be written in white on one of the many mirrors or on strategically placed blackboards.

Une brasserie

Many *brasseries*, especially in Paris and larger cities, will have a special display of seafood, particularly oysters, on an outside counter near the entrance. There will be *un écailler*, an oyster seller, opening the oysters as he receives orders from inside.

Brasseries, unlike many restaurants, are open seven days a week, have flexible hours and will take orders even at ten or eleven o'clock in the evening. They open early and do not usually close between the lunchtime and evening service. In off-peak hours, they will serve a reduced choice of dishes or have tables available for people who just wish to have a coffee or a beer.

Brasseries will usually have some regional dishes on the menu and often typical dishes from Alsace.

AT LUNCHTIME, PARTICULARLY, MANY *BRASSERIES* HAVE SEVERAL COMBINATIONS SO THAT BUSY PEOPLE CAN ORDER JUST A STARTER, A MAIN COURSE AND A COFFEE, OR A MAIN COURSE AND DESSERT.

As you enter, you will be greeted and your reservation will be checked (it is usually essential to reserve in advance at the bigger, well-known *brasseries*) and you will be led to your table and given a menu. The waiters will be smartly dressed in long-sleeved white shirts and black waistcoats and trousers. They will often have a white teacloth placed over one shoulder. Head waiters, who have a red-backed waistcoat or other distinguishing sign, will be responsible for checking that all is well and for bringing the bill at the end of your meal.

🔊 KEYWORDS

une réservation	reservation
un serveur	waiter
un chef de rang	head waiter
une banquette	(wall) seat
le comptoir	bar
une bière blonde	lager
une bière brune	brown ale
une pression	draught beer
un demi	half a pint (25cl)
l'eau plate	still water
l'eau pétillante	sparkling water
une carafe d'eau	tap water
une entrée	starter
le plat principal	main course
un steak frites	steak and chips
un steak tartare	steak tartare
une choucroute	sauerkraut (served with meat)
les huîtres	oysters
l'addition	bill

Une brasserie

After placing your order, you will be able to watch the waiters as they carry heavily laden circular trays, which they balance on one hand and hold high in the air. Arriving at your table, they may use their free hand to open a small stand on which they position the tray while they serve the individual dishes. This small table is then folded and stacked to allow other waiters to pass. It takes a lot of experience to serve clients quickly and efficiently in the busy, crowded environment of a *brasserie*. It is also physically very demanding.

Serving in a well-known *brasserie* is, however, considered to be an important professional experience and many waiters will spend several years, or even their entire careers, in a prestigious *brasserie*.

In the evening, meals are a more leisurely experience, with menus based upon traditional dishes such as a *choucroute*, a *steak frites* or a *steak tartare*. Servings are usually generous. Some of the lunch-time formula combinations may not be available in the evenings, and the average price of a meal may be higher, especially in renowned establishments.

If you don't have time for a meal in a *brasserie*, stop by for a hot chocolate between four and five o'clock. You will have the opportunity to admire the historical setting and understand why these bustling establishments have been a feature of French and particularly Parisian life for so long.

Nos grandes Assiettes

• L'assiette Campagnarde	13,90
• L'assiette vigneronne	14,30

Les viandes

• Le faux filet grillé aux herbes de Provence	13,60
• Le Carpaccio de boeuf	13,20
• Le tartare de boeuf	14,10
• La cuisse de canard confite	14,60

Nos Assiettes végétariennes

• Le gratin de légume aux ravioles de Royans	
• La tarte salée	11,10
• La lasagne de légumes	11,30
• Le Saint Marcellin rôti à l'ail	11,60
	12,60

Nos marmites de moules et frites

• La Gibraltar (ail, vin blanc)	12,80
• La Havre (crème, échalotes)	12,80
• L'Essaouira (à l'orientale)	12,90
• La Bora Bora (moutarde à l'ancienne)	12,90
• La Bombay (au curry, des Indes)	12,90

Carte de vins, bières à la pression, Soirées musicales.

Une brasserie

HISTORY AND TRADITIONS

A _brasserie_ was originally a place where beer was brewed. It later became the name of places where drinks, especially beer, and quickly prepared meals were served. Many _brasseries_ originated in Alsace, or were created by Alsatian immigrants, or supplied by Alsatian brewers. After the war of 1870 when Germany annexed Alsace, most of the beer came from Lorraine.

Many famous _brasseries_ are still linked to their original Alsatian owners by their names and special traditions. La Brasserie Georges in Lyon carries on many of the traditions introduced by its founder. It is known for its _choucroute_, a typical Alsatian dish. It even claims the world record for the biggest _choucroute_ ever served and, at 34 metres, the longest Norwegian Omelette, its signature ice-cream dessert topped with meringue.

CULTURAL TIPS

You are not required to leave a tip in a _brasserie_ although a tip is always appreciated. It can range from any loose change you have received when you paid to 10 or 15% of the bill.

The toilets are often found down a winding staircase. There may be separate toilets for men and women, but not necessarily in smaller establishments. In the past, clients would go down the stairs to the basement, _le sous-sol_, to use the telephone, as this was where it was situated. People wishing to use the telephone would enter a _brasserie_ and pay for a _jeton_ (a metal chip) at the bar counter to enable them to make their call. Some _brasseries_ have kept these phones in place as reminders of their past.

🔊 USEFUL PHRASES

— _Une table pour deux, s'il vous plaît._
   A table for two, please.
— _Je prends le menu du jour, s'il vous plaît._
   I'll have today's special, please.
— _Je prends un plat et un dessert, s'il vous plaît._
   I'll have a main course and a dessert, please.
— _Je prends le poulet et une mousse au chocolat, s'il vous plaît._
   I'll have the chicken and the chocolate mousse, please.
— _Et une demi-bouteille d'eau pétillante, s'il vous plaît._
   And a half-bottle of sparkling water, please.
— _Pas de café, merci._
   No coffee, thanks.
— _Où sont les toilettes, s'il vous plaît ?_
   Where are the toilets/restrooms, please?
— _Je peux avoir l'addition, s'il vous plaît ?_
   Can I have the bill/check, please?
— _Un chocolat chaud, s'il vous plaît._
   A hot chocolate, please.

Une brasserie

Even today, beer will often accompany a meal in a *brasserie*, although most brasseries now also have a wine list.

As *brasseries* are usually large establishments, families and groups of friends often choose them to celebrate a special occasion such as a birthday. When the dessert, which may be decorated with candles, arrives, several waiters will gather around and sing 'Happy Birthday', or rather, *'Bon anniversaire'*. Occasionally a traditional barrel organ will be brought alongside the table and a waiter will turn the instrument's handle to accompany the singing with music. It is customary for everybody in the room to clap at the end. Tradition and a noisy, friendly atmosphere are very much part of the *brasserie* experience.

🔊 *Remember*

If you just want a drink, you should check that this is possible before being seated:
– *Je peux juste prendre quelque chose à boire ?*
Can I just have something to drink?

At busy times you may be directed to the bar counter rather than a table.

Coffee is always served after the dessert in France. If you want it at the same time as the dessert, you will need to request this.
– *Vous pouvez servir le café avec le dessert, s'il vous plaît ? Nous sommes pressés.*
Could we have our coffee with the dessert, please? We're in a hurry.

🔊 YOU WILL HEAR

– *Suivez-moi, s'il vous plaît.*
Please follow me.
– *Vous avez fait votre choix ?*
Are you ready to order?
– *Qu'est-ce que vous voulez boire ?*
What would you like to drink?
– *Attention, l'assiette est très chaude.*
Careful, the plate is very hot.
– *Tout se passe bien ?*
Everything all right?
– *Vous avez terminé ?*
Have you finished?
– *Vous voulez un dessert ?*
Would you like a dessert?
– *Vous prenez un café ?*
Do you want a coffee?

Une brasserie

🔊 LANGUAGE TIPS

When your waiter asks you if you want a dessert or more wine, you can simply reply *"Merci"*, if you wish to refuse. In the case of wine, you can accompany this with a gesture. Hold your open hand, palm down, just over your wine glass.

In the noise and bustle of a *brasserie*, you may find it particularly difficult to hear and understand what is being said to you.
Try to prepare what you need to say so that you can concentrate on the reply. If you don't hear something, you can say:
– *Vous pouvez répéter, s'il vous plaît ?*
Could you repeat that, please?
– *Excusez-moi. Je n'ai pas entendu.*
I'm sorry, I didn't hear that.

🔊 ADVANCED USEFUL PHRASES

– *C'est possible de prendre la table près de la fenêtre ?*
Is it possible to have the table near the window?
– *Désolé, nous n'avons pas encore décidé.*
Sorry, we haven't made up our minds yet.
– *J'ai besoin d'une explication, s'il vous plaît.*
I need an explanation, please.
– *Qu'est-ce qu'une brandade de morue ?*
What is a cod brandade?
– *Est-ce que vous avez des plats végétariens, s'il vous plaît ?*
Do you have any vegetarian dishes, please?
– *Je crois qu'il y a une erreur dans ma commande.*
I think my order is wrong.
– *Vous pouvez nous apporter du pain, s'il vous plaît ?*
Could you bring us some bread, please?
– *Qu'est-ce que vous avez comme dessert ?*
What desserts do you have?
– *Vous pouvez nous faire des notes séparées, s'il vous plaît ?*
Could you give us separate bills, please?

 **LEARN MORE**

You can find more examples of ordering dishes in French in *Un restaurant*, p.22.

To specify the sort of coffee you prefer, you can refer to *Un café*, p.8.

Une brasserie

Most famous

Over the years, some of the most famous *brasseries*, each with spectacular ornate interiors, have been:

– La Coupole (Paris). Famous artists and writers including Picasso, Matisse, Henry Miller, James Joyce and Jean-Paul Sartre dined here, and Albert Camus celebrated his Nobel Prize at his usual table.

– La Brasserie Georges (Lyon) serves on average 700 diners per service with a peak of 2,500 on the evenings of the Fête des lumières in December.

– Brasserie Lipp (Paris) was created in 1880 and is situated in the historic Saint-Germain-des-Prés district and counts artists of the cinema and stage, writers and politicians among its clients.

There are also many other reputed establishments, such as:

– Les Deux Magots (Paris)
– Le Bœuf sur le Toit (Paris)
– Brasserie Flo (Paris)
– Brasserie Wepler (Paris)
– Brasserie Flo "Les Beaux Arts" (Toulouse)

Also popular are the newer large *brasseries* established by world-famous chef, Paul Bocuse, in Lyon: Le Sud, Le Nord, L'Est et L'Ouest, which reflect regional cuisines.

Quiz

Are the following statements true or false?

A. In a *brasserie*, you can only drink beer.
   ☐ True   ☐ False

B. *Brasseries* are small and intimate.
   ☐ True   ☐ False

C. *Brasseries* have lots of menu choices.
   ☐ True   ☐ False

D. *Brasseries* are open every day.
   ☐ True   ☐ False

E. *Brasseries* are very formal.
   ☐ True   ☐ False

F. You can order just a main course, if you wish, in a *brasserie*.
   ☐ True   ☐ False

Answers: A. False, B. False, C. True, D. True, E. False, F. True.

KEY POINTS

Brasseries...

- have flexible hours and serve late in the evening.
- often have elaborately styled dining areas.
- serve simple, traditional dishes.
- are generally good value for money.
- are part of a long French tradition.

Un restaurant

WHAT TO EXPECT

The menu is placed in your hands, the wine list is placed on the table and you are invited to order an *apéritif*. Relish this moment as anticipation is part of the pleasure when dining in a French *restaurant*. Should you order *à la carte* or choose a set menu? Should you let yourself be tempted by the *menu du marché* with its seasonal specialities or do you want to discover the region's delicacies with a *menu dégustation*?

If you find it difficult to choose, you can enlist the help of the person taking your order. Even French people sometimes need explanations concerning a particular dish and its preparation. The wine waiter will also be there to suggest which wine will best accompany your meal. He will give you any information you may require concerning the selection of wines from France's many wine-producing regions.

CULTURAL TIPS

In most *restaurants*, you will be able to order a carafe of house wine, which is less expensive than a bottle of wine. Wine by the glass is becoming more common, but is still not widespread.

If you select the cheese course, you can choose between the cheeseboard and *un fromage blanc*. The latter is a smooth mixture of drained milk curds, served with cream, to which you can add sugar. If you decide on the cheeseboard, you will be brought a knife and fork so you can cut the rind off certain cheeses. Note that a Camembert cheese is eaten with the rind.

ANTICIPATION IS PART OF THE PLEASURE WHEN DINING IN A FRENCH *RESTAURANT*.

Un restaurant

With your *apéritif*, your waiter will probably bring olives, nuts or an olive paste called *tapenade* and toasted bread. In more sophisticated *restaurants*, there will be a dainty dish with something colourful and intriguing before the first course. This is what the French call *un amuse-bouche*, literally something to amuse your mouth. It is a promise of what is to come.

As you eat your starter and then the main course, you can take your time and appreciate the presentation and taste of the food. Your waiter will check that everything is to your liking and watch for when you are ready for the table to be cleared after each course.

In France it is customary to spend time over a meal, particularly an evening meal out. If you are with French people, be prepared to discuss the different dishes in some detail. French people have strong views on food and love talking about it.

◀)) **KEY**WORDS

l'entrée	starter
le plat principal	main course
le pain	bread
la viande	meat
le poisson	fish
les légumes	vegetables
le plateau de fromages	cheeseboard
le chariot des desserts	dessert trolley
le vin rouge	red wine
le vin blanc	white wine
le vin rosé	rosé wine
une carafe d'eau	a jug of water
un pichet de vin	a carafe of wine
une infusion	herbal tea
un digestif	liqueur
un couteau	knife
une fourchette	fork
une cuillère	spoon

Un restaurant

Until recently, French *restaurants* used to serve cheese and then dessert. Nowadays, you will find both only on more expensive fixed menus. If you opt for the cheeseboard, a selection of cheeses will be brought to you on a plate, or you will be able to choose from the cheese trolley. The cheeses you select will be placed around your plate in the order in which you should eat them, moving from milder to stronger-tasting cheeses.

Dessert will follow and you will be able to enjoy a classic French dessert or discover one of the chef's creations. Later in the evening, you may even have the opportunity to meet the chef. His work in the kitchen done, he will come to each table and greet everyone.

Then it's time for a coffee served with little cakes, chocolates or small meringues, *des mignardises*, to round off the evening and complete your gourmet experience.

IN FRANCE IT IS CUSTOMARY TO SPEND TIME OVER A MEAL, PARTICULARLY AN EVENING MEAL OUT.

CULTURAL TIPS

It will surprise a waiter if you order a coffee with milk or cream at the end of your meal. The French consider this difficult to digest and only drink black coffee or, alternatively, a herbal tea after eating. Sometimes they will also order a liqueur, *un digestif*, mockingly referred to as *un pousse-café*, something that follows the coffee and therefore pushes it down.

It is always best to reserve a table, particularly at a well-known *restaurant*. The evening service will not begin before seven thirty or sometimes eight o'clock in Paris. People usually eat late in French cities, particularly Paris, but in rural areas, *restaurants* may not accept customers after nine o'clock.

In French *restaurants*, you will be brought a basket with bread and a carafe of tap water (unless you order bottled water). This is included in the price of your meal.

Un restaurant

HISTORY AND TRADITIONS

Legend has it that the Tour d'argent in Paris, founded in 1582, was the first French *restaurant*, but generally, during the 16th and 17th centuries, *restaurants* were places where just meat broth was served. Broth was seen as something which restored people's strength, and so the word *restaurant* comes from the French word *restaurer*, to restore.

In 1782, La Grande Taverne de Londres opened and the tradition of great Parisian *restaurants* was established. The number of *restaurants* increased after the Revolution when, as the aristocracy had fled the capital, many cooks and waiters found themselves without work and established their own *restaurants*.

◀》 USEFUL PHRASES

– *J'ai réservé une table pour quatre personnes.*
I reserved a table for four.
– *Nous allons prendre le menu à 40 euros, s'il vous plaît.*
We'll take the 40-euros menu, please.
– *C'est servi avec quels légumes, s'il vous plaît ?*
Which vegetables does it come with, please?
– *Je prendrai la terrine de canard suivie par le saumon, s'il vous plaît.*
I'll have the duck pâté and then the salmon, please.
– *Qu'est-ce que vous suggérez comme vin ?*
Which wine would you recommend?
– *Je prendrai une infusion, s'il vous plaît. Vous avez du tilleul ?*
I'll have a herbal tea, please. Do you have lime-blossom tea?
– *Vous pouvez nous apporter l'addition, s'il vous plaît ?*
Can you bring us the bill, please?
– *Le repas était très bon.*
It was a very good meal.

◀》 IDIOMS

– *Aimer les plaisirs de la table* means to enjoy one's food.
– *Manger comme un cochon* is to eat like a pig.
– *Ça ne mange pas de pain* means it doesn't cost much.
– *Il boit du petit lait* means he's as pleased as Punch.
– *Il y a à boire et à manger là-dedans* means it has its good and its bad points.

Un restaurant

In the 19th century, many more *restaurants* opened to serve workers and craftsmen too, and soon articles about good *restaurants* started to appear in the press. Michelin, the tyre company, produced LE GUIDE ROUGE in 1900 to help people travelling by car, and in 1920 it included *restaurants* for the first time. It became very popular and the famous three-star rating system was introduced in 1931.

Today, if you want to choose a good *restaurant* in France, the number of Michelin stars it is attributed can still guide you. For a lower budget, you can also look for *restaurants* with the Logis de France label. Or, you can just wander around and make your own choice by reading the menus displayed. The good thing about France is that even modest *restaurants* can still delight you with excellent food.

THE 41 PAINTINGS ON THE WALLS AND CEILINGS OF THE FAMOUS LE TRAIN BLEU *RESTAURANT* IN PARIS ARE ADMIRED BY MORE THAN 500 DINERS EVERY DAY.

CULTURAL TIPS

Most *restaurant* prices are now TTC, *toutes taxes comprises*. The price on the menu usually includes a service charge as well as any taxes. In the past these were added to your bill at the end. You can still leave a tip, as this is always appreciated, but there is no fixed percentage. In expensive *restaurants*, only the menu of the person who has reserved the table will have the prices marked on it.

It is considered good manners in France to keep your hands resting on the table when you are not eating. It is also customary to keep your fork in your left hand. However, manners are becoming more relaxed and it is noticeable that people do not dress up as much for a meal out as in the past.

YOU WILL HEAR

– *Vous avez réservé ?*
Did you reserve?
– *Je peux prendre votre manteau ?*
Can I take your coat?
– *Vous êtes prêts à passer votre commande ?*
Are you ready to order?
– *Quelle cuisson pour la viande ? Bien cuite ou rosée ?*
How do you like your meat cooked? Well-done or rare?
– *Vous avez choisi votre vin ?*
Have you chosen your wine?

– *Je vous souhaite bon appétit.*
Enjoy your meal.
– *Je peux débarrasser ?*
Can I clear the table?
– *Qu'est-ce que vous souhaitez prendre pour le dessert ?*
What would you like for dessert?
– *Je vous propose un petit digestif ?*
Can I suggest a liqueur?
– *Je vous souhaite une très bonne fin de soirée.*
Have an excellent evening.

Un restaurant

 LANGUAGE TIPS

When your waiter brings your order to the table, he will probably know which dish is for each person. However, if he has a doubt, he will say the name of the dish, at which point you can say:
– *Le poisson, c'est pour moi.*
The fish is for me.

If you are not able to finish your dish, you can say:
– *C'était très bon, mais je suis désolé, je ne peux pas finir.*
It was very good, but I'm sorry, I can't finish.

When the waiter brings your first dish, he will say:
– *Bon appétit !*
Enjoy your meal!

For the following dishes or the dessert, you may hear him say:
– *Bonne continuation !*
Continue to enjoy your meal!

Remember

Most *restaurants* will remove your knife and fork after each course and bring you clean ones. In some *restaurants*, however, you may be asked to keep them:
– *Gardez votre couteau et votre fourchette, s'il vous plaît.*
Please keep your knife and fork.

When you have finished a course and want to signal this to your waiter, you should leave your knife and fork crossed at right angles on your plate. When you are just pausing, place your knife and fork on each side of the plate with the handles resting on the table.

DINING IN
TOULOUSE

 LEARN MORE

You can find more examples of ordering food in *Une brasserie*, p.15.

For other examples of asking for more information, you can refer to *Une fromagerie*, p.52.

Un restaurant

Most famous

La Maison Troisgros in Roanne was established in 1930 by Jean-Baptiste and Marie Troisgros. Their sons, who shared their parents' passion for good food and wine, earned a Michelin star. In 1965, the brothers gained a second star, and shortly afterward a third. They became, with other chefs, founders of *la nouvelle cuisine*. The restaurant has kept its three Michelin stars for more than 40 years and is considered one of the best in the world.

Anne-Sophie Pic is the only female chef in France with a three-star Michelin rating. Her *restaurant* in Valence, simply called Pic, is also the fruit of a long family tradition stretching over three generations. Her cuisine is based upon simplicity and flavour.

Paul Bocuse has undoubtedly contributed more than any other French chef to the worldwide reputation of French cooking. His restaurant L'Auberge du pont de Collonges near Lyon was one of the first *restaurants* to earn three Michelin stars. It is a place of pilgrimage for everyone who loves French food.

Among the many other exceptional *restaurants* in France are those of Alain Ducasse in Monte-Carlo and Paris and the *restaurant* created by Bernard Loiseau at Saulieu.

Match the first half of the sentence with its second half.

A. *J'ai réservé une table...*	**1.** *très bon.*
B. *Vous avez un vin...*	**2.** *l'addition s'il vous plaît ?*
C. *Non, pas de café...*	**3.** *pour quatre.*
D. *Je prendrai...*	**4.** *pour moi.*
E. *Le repas était...*	**5.** *de la région ?*
F. *Vous pouvez nous apporter...*	**6.** *le menu à 30 euros.*

Answers: A3, B5, C4, D6, E1, F2.

🔊 ADVANCED USEFUL PHRASES

– *C'est possible de manger en terrasse ?*
Would it be possible to eat outside?
– *Quels sont les plats traditionnels de la région ?*
What are the traditional dishes of the region?
– *Je préfère la viande bien cuite, s'il vous plaît.*
I prefer my meat well-done, please.
– *Est-ce que vous avez des demi-bouteilles de vin ?*
Do you have half bottles of wine?
– *Excusez-moi, mais le poisson était pour moi.*
Excuse me, but the fish is for me.
– *Donnez-moi un peu de ce fromage-là, s'il vous plaît et puis un peu de ce bleu.*
I'll have a bit of that cheese, please, and then a little of this blue cheese.
– *Je prendrai bien un digestif. Qu'est-ce que vous avez ?*
I think I'll have a liqueur. What do you have?
– *Il faut que j'aille au bar pour régler avec la carte ?*
Do I need to go to the bar to pay with a credit card?

KEY POINTS

Restaurants...

● start their evening service at seven thirty or later.
● sometimes serve wine by the glass, but often only by the bottle.
● may offer a choice of a cheese course or a dessert.
● have fixed menus and dishes *à la carte*.
● include service and taxes in the menu price, but you can add a tip if you wish.

Une crêperie, un bouchon…

Une crêperie, un bouchon…

WHAT TO EXPECT

No wonder France is the world's top tourist destination. Travel its length and breadth and you will be astonished by the changes in the landscape and the houses. French regional cooking reflects this tremendous variety. Go into a *crêperie* in Brittany and a *bouchon* in Lyon and you would be justified in thinking you were in two different countries.

Simplicity and informality are the characteristics of France's many traditional regional restaurants. The décor evokes local trades or local history, the ambiance is relaxed, and above all, the food is a celebration of regional specialities.

Brittany is the home of *crêperies*, *restaurants* serving *crêpes*, thin pancakes with lacelike edges. A typical *crêperie* is often painted in Breton blue and the furniture is simple: wooden tables, sometimes with benches rather than chairs. The menu will have a large selection of *crêpes bretonnes*. You can choose between *crêpes* made from buckwheat flour, often called *galettes* and associated with savoury fillings, or wheat flour *crêpes* with a sweet filling. The *crêpe* will be served on its own, or sometimes with a side salad, and you can your savoury *crêpe* with a sweet *crêpe* for dessert. *Crêpes* are traditionally accompanied by apple cider poured into small earthenware bowls rather than glasses.

CULTURAL TIPS

In a *crêperie*, you can choose between *crêpes* made with wheat flour (*les crêpes au froment*) which are normally sweet, and those made from buckwheat flour, *les crêpes au sarrasin*, or *les crêpes au blé noir*, which are savoury. In certain parts of Brittany, *crêpes* made with buckwheat are also called *galettes*. Traditionally, a little salted butter is placed on top just before serving.

Une crêperie, un bouchon...

Travel down to Lyon in the southeast of France and, among the city's many famous *restaurants*, you will find some known as *bouchons*. Usually small, with lots of wood and traditional red and white checkered tablecloths, *bouchons* are intimate and friendly establishments. You may need some help to understand the menu, but don't worry, so will many French people. *Bouchons* serve Lyon's traditional dishes based on pork and beef, including the famous *tablier de sapeur* made from cow's stomach. Portions are usually large and you can accompany your meal with a traditional *pot* of Beaujolais wine.

CULTURAL TIPS

In a *bouchon lyonnais*, you can discover specialities such as *quenelles* (a mixture of flour and ground fish cooked like a soufflé), kidneys, sweetbread and *andouillettes*, a sort of sausage. You can also try the famous *tablier de sapeur*, a dish made from tripe. If you are not sure whether these traditional Lyon dishes are to your taste, you can order something more familiar instead. The ambiance of a *bouchon* is not to be missed, however.

SIMPLICITY AND INFORMALITY ARE THE CHARACTERISTICS OF FRANCE'S MANY TRADITIONAL REGIONAL *RESTAURANTS*.

Une crêperie, un bouchon...

FERMES-AUBERGES WILL
SERVE DUCK AND GEESE.

As you approach the Mediterranean, you will find the colourful vegetables of the local markets on your plate in the many typical Provençal *restaurants*. Along the coast itself, seafood *restaurants* abound and you can choose between elaborate dishes of oysters, crayfish and lobster, or simple, tasty bowls of mussels. And of course, don't miss the traditional *bouillabaisse*, Marseille's famous fish soup.

Head across to the southwest of France and you will find another region with rich gastronomic traditions. *Fermes-auberges* will serve duck and geese and endless varieties of pâtés, including *foie gras*. You will of course have to double back to take in the cheese dishes of the Jura and Alps, eaten in wooden chalets after a day's skiing. And you will have only just begun to understand the variety of France's traditional regional *restaurants* — one of the reasons, no doubt, why France continues to attract so many visitors year after year.

KEYWORDS

une crêpe	thin pancake
une crêpe au sucre	crêpe sprinkled with sugar
une bolée de cidre	bowl(ful) of cider
la cochonnaille	foodstuffs made from pork
les rognons	kidneys
le ris de veau	calf's sweetbread
un pot de beaujolais	thick-bottomed glass bottle filled with Beaujolais wine
des moules-frites	mussels and chips/French fries
des fruits de mer	seafood
une bouillabaisse	Provençal fish soup
une huître	oyster
un magret de canard	duck breast
un confit d'oie	conserve of goose
un cassoulet	stew of beans and duck or pork
une raclette	melted cheese served with potatoes and cold meats
une fondue	(cheese) fondue
une nappe à carreaux	checkered tablecloth
un verre	glass
un banc	bench

IDIOMS

– *Un canard* is a duck, but also a sugar lump dipped in coffee.
– *Retourner quelqu'un comme une crêpe* means to change someone's mind easily.
– *Pousser le bouchon un peu loin* means to go a bit far.
– *Se fermer comme une huître* means to clam up.

Une crêperie, un bouchon...

HISTORY AND TRADITIONS

The *bouchons lyonnais* can be traced back to the old coaching houses or post inns, places where drivers could eat and drink while their horses were cleaned and fed. The innkeepers would hang a bundle of branches with pine cones on their door, an allusion to Bacchus, to show they sold wine. In the local dialect, this bundle was called a *bousche* and the inns became known as *bouchons*.

As Lyon's silk industry prospered, *bouchons* also became places where the silk workers ate. After an early start, they traditionally took a break around nine o'clock when they ate a meal known as *un mâchon*. These simple, inexpensive but hearty meals were often based on parts of animals not considered good enough for the bourgeois classes. Usually the innkeeper's wife cooked while the innkeeper served and created a lively atmosphere in the eating area.

CULTURAL TIPS

You may be surprised to see *la cervelle de canut* among the desserts in a *bouchon Lyonnais*. It has nothing to do with the literal meaning of *une cervelle*, which is brains. This dessert is made from drained milk curds, beaten and seasoned with garlic, chives, parsley, salt and pepper. The workers in Lyon's famous silk industry were called *les Canuts*.

If you enjoy regional cooking when in France, look out for *fermes-auberges*. These are country inns, run by farmers, serving meals based on farm produce. They have a simple setting, a friendly, relaxed atmosphere and an emphasis on local dishes.

🔊 USEFUL PHRASES

— *Qu'est-ce que c'est ?*
  What is that?
— *Quelle est la spécialité régionale ?*
  What's the local speciality?
— *Ça se mange comment ?*
  How do you eat it?
— *C'est très copieux ?*
  Is it a very generous portion?
— *C'est très épicé ?*
  Is it very spicy?
— *C'est servi avec des légumes ?*
  Are there vegetables with it?
— *Je vais essayer les quenelles.*
  I'm going to try the quenelles.
— *Je veux bien essayer le cassoulet.*
  I'll give the cassoulet a go.
— *Je prendrai des moules-frites, s'il vous plaît.*
  I'll have mussels and chips/French fries, please.
— *Je prends du cidre, s'il vous plaît.*
  I'll have cider, please.

Une crêperie, un bouchon...

IN LYON'S HISTORIC DISTRICT, *BOUCHONS* ARE HIDDEN IN THE QUIET SIDE STREETS.

Crêpes were also traditionally eaten by the poorer classes. Buckwheat flour, cultivated in Brittany following its introduction from Asia after the Crusades, was used to make *crêpes*. Cooked on a single hot stone, *crêpes* were a meal in themselves. Sometimes they were broken into pieces and added to bowls of cider. It was only from the early 20th century that *crêpes* were also made with wheat flour.

Les fermes-auberges are linked to the long tradition of moving animals up into the mountains to summer pastures. The farmers lived for this period in small farms where they often also made cheese. In the 19th century, they began to offer simple hospitality to walkers and hikers. As the meals proposed became more varied, the farmers opened veritable *auberges*, or country inns. The idea spread to other parts of rural France and the tradition of *les fermes-auberges* was born.

🔊 *Remember*

When eating in a *bouchon lyonnais* or around Lyon, you can order a traditional *pot* of wine. This is a glass bottle with a thick base, which holds 46 centilitres. The wine will be either a Beaujolais wine or a Côtes du Rhône. You can say:
– *Je prends un pot de beaujolais, s'il vous plaît.*

In Savoy, a popular dish after a day's skiing is a *fondue*. Made from white wine, garlic, cornflour and grated local cheeses, the *fondue* is placed in the centre of the table on a burner. A long fork allows you to dip a piece of bread in the mixture and carry it to your mouth. Be careful though: if you drop the bread in the *fondue*, you will have *un gage*, a penalty, such as having to sing or dance!

🔊 YOU WILL HEAR

– *Vous voulez une crêpe au froment ou au sarrasin ?*
Do you want a crêpe made with wheat flour or with buckwheat flour?
– *Du cidre doux ou brut ?*
Sweet or dry cider?
– *Nous avons plusieurs plats régionaux.*
We have several regional dishes.
– *C'est un plat à base de poisson.*
It's a fish dish.
– *Vous verrez, c'est très bon.*
You'll see, it's very good.
– *Il faut aimer. C'est un peu particulier.*
It's not to everyone's taste. It's a bit unusual.
– *C'est servi avec du riz et une sauce madère.*
It comes with rice and a Madeira wine sauce.
– *Les frites sont à volonté.*
You can have as many chips/French fries as you like.

Une crêperie, un bouchon...

🔊 LANGUAGE TIPS

Since a *ferme-auberge* or a *crêperie* often serve groups or families, they may ask you when you arrive:
– *C'est pour combien ?*
For how many?

If you don't know where to find a traditional *bouchon lyonnais*, a *crêperie* or a *ferme-auberge* in a particular town or region, you can ask at the local *office de tourisme*:
– *Vous pouvez me recommander un bouchon lyonnais ?*
Can you give me the name of a *bouchon lyonnais* ?

Even if they can't recommend one specifically, they will be able to give you some names and show you where they are on a map.

CULTURAL TIPS

You will often see the words *produits du terroir* in restaurants. The concept of *terroir* is very important to the French, particularly in relation to wine and food. It literally means soil, but by extension means something that is local or specific to a certain region.

Seafood is highly prized in France and along the coasts there are many restaurants specialising in crabs, lobsters, oysters, mussels, crayfish and prawns, to name just a few of the delicacies you will find on a *plateau de fruits de mer*.

The French always used to say that you should eat oysters only in months that have the letter 'R' in their names. This excluded the hot summer months from May to August. Nowadays, with improved specialised transport, you will see French people enjoying oysters all year round, although the peak in sales remains the end-of-year holiday season.

🕊 LEARN MORE

You can find more examples of asking for more information in *Une fromagerie*, p.52.

You can refer to *Une brasserie*, p.15 and *Un restaurant*, p.22 for further examples of ordering food.

Une crêperie, un bouchon...

Most famous

Bouchons have contributed to Lyon's reputation as one of the world's top gastronomic destinations. Today more than 20 restaurants are classified as authentic *bouchons lyonnais*.

Among them are Le Garet, one of the oldest *bouchons*. Chez Georges has just a few tables, huge serving bowls and an animated atmosphere. Daniel et Denise has won many awards. Not to be forgotten is Le Mâchon, named after that hearty early morning meal enjoyed by Lyon's silk workers.

Crêpes remain a regional speciality, although with the flow of emigrants from Brittany in the mid-20th century, several *crêperies bretonnes* have opened in Paris and across France, as well as in other countries.

Most rural regions of France have some *fermes-auberges*. To choose a *ferme-auberge* or *crêperie*, it is best to consult a local tourist office.

🔊 ADVANCED USEFUL PHRASES

– Vous pouvez m'expliquer un peu comment ce plat est preparé, s'il vous plaît ?
Can you explain a little about how this dish is prepared, please?
– Ça se fait uniquement dans cette région ?
Is it made only in this area?
– Est-ce que c'est possible de commander cette crêpe mais sans les champignons, s'il vous plaît ?
Would it be possible to order this crêpe, but without the mushrooms, please?
– Quel vin se marie bien avec ce plat ?
Which wine would go well with this dish?
– C'est vous qui êtes à l'origine de cette ferme-auberge ?
Did you start this ferme-auberge?
– Est-ce que tout vient de votre exploitation ?
Is everything produced on the farm?
– Vous pouvez m'indiquer un restaurant qui se spécialise dans la cuisine régionale ?
Can you give me the name of a restaurant specialising in regional cooking?
– Je voudrais essayer des plats régionaux. Où vaut-il mieux aller ?
I'd like to try some regional dishes. Where's the best place to go?

Circle the words that don't belong.

A. *le froment, le blé noir, le riz, le sarrasin*

B. *le canard, le confit, le foie gras, la raclette*

C. *la cervelle de canut, le cassoulet, la fondue, la bouillabaisse*

D. *la bolée, le pot, un verre, un plat*

E. *un homard, un magret, une langouste, une huître*

D. *les quenelles, les moules, les andouillettes, les rognons*

Answers: A. *le riz* (not an ingredient of *crêpes*). B. *la raclette* (not associated with the southwest of France). C. *la cervelle de canut* (a dessert, not a main course). D. *un plat* (not a container for drinks). E. *un magret* (meat, not seafood). F. *les moules* (not traditionally on the menu of a *bouchon lyonnais*).

▮ KEY POINTS

Crêperies, bouchons lyonnais...

● demonstrate the variety of France's regional cuisines.
● serve traditional, local specialities.
● have an informal atmosphere.
● reflect a region's history.
● are part of the French concept of *terroir*.

As they say in French

- « *L'appétit vient en mangeant.* »
  Proverbe français

- « *Le mariage est comme le restaurant : à peine est-on servi qu'on regarde ce qu'il y a dans l'assiette du voisin.* »
  Sacha Guitry

- « *Il faut manger pour vivre et non pas vivre pour manger.* »
  Molière

- « *La gastronomie est l'art d'utiliser la nourriture pour créer le bonheur.* »
  Theodore Zeldin

- « *Cuisiner suppose une tête légère, un esprit généreux et un cœur large.* »
  Paul Gaugin

- « *Bonne cuisine et bon vin, c'est le paradis sur terre.* »
  Henri IV

Part 2

TRADITIONAL FOOD SHOPS

Une boulangerie

WHAT TO EXPECT

A man on a bike, wearing a *béret*, with a *baguette* under his arm. This image of the typical Frenchman may be an outdated stereotype, but all over the world the *baguette* remains emblematic of France.

Pause for a sandwich in a *café* anywhere in France, and more likely than not, it will arrive in the form of half a *baguette*, cut lengthways, with the filling of your choice. A meal in a typical *restaurant* will usually be preceded by the arrival of a bread basket filled with cut portions of *baguette*. And of course, you will often see French people making their way home carrying a crusty *baguette* or two.

CULTURAL TIPS

As well as bread, most *boulangeries* will also sell a variety of *viennoiseries* including *croissants, pains au chocolat* and *pains aux raisins,* and generally small quiches and slices of pizzas, too.

A *boulangerie* that also sells cakes is called a *boulangerie-pâtisserie.* However a *pâtisserie* can not normally sell bread.

When buying bread in France you can ask for it to be sliced, choose a loaf that is more or less baked, or buy just a portion of a large loaf.

A *baguette* is 60 centimetres long and weighs 250 grams. It is a sign of quality if, when you press a *baguette*, it springs back into shape. Traditionally the *baguette* was Parisian but nowadays it is available all over France. Many myths abide as to its origin but no one really knows.

A FRENCH PERSON MAY BUY HIS BREAD FROM A GIVEN *BOULANGERIE* BECAUSE IT IS THE ONLY ONE IN HIS SMALL VILLAGE BUT, WHEN POSSIBLE, HE WILL MAKE HIS WAY TO THE *BOULANGERIE* WHERE THE BREAD IS TO HIS TASTE.

Une boulangerie

Go into a French *boulangerie* anywhere in France and you will inevitably see these famous *baguettes*, stacked vertically to accommodate their length. You will also be presented with a variety of other breads, some traditional, some regional and some the signature of a particular baker. The choice and the need for a specific vocabulary can seem overwhelming. How to ask for that loaf where the dough has been braided? Is it possible to request just a part of that enormous long loaf lying temptingly on the counter? Other than shape or size, what are the criteria for choice?

A French person may buy his bread from a given *boulangerie* because it is the only one in his small village but, when possible, he will make his way to the *boulangerie* where the bread is to his taste. For a French person, bread is an important element in a meal and strong preferences for a specific form of loaf with a given consistency and a certain degree of crustiness are common. In August, when many *boulangeries* close, Parisians often lament that they have to walk considerable distances to find the kind of bread they prefer.

◀》 KEYWORDS

une baguette	baguette/French stick
un pain complet	wholemeal/whole wheat loaf
un pain de mie	sandwich bread
un pain de campagne	farmhouse bread
un pain de seigle	rye bread
un pain aux raisins	Danish pastry
un croissant aux amandes	almond croissant
une tarte aux pommes	apple tart
une fournée	batch
un pain en tranches	sliced loaf
la croûte	crust
bien cuit	crisp
un sandwich au jambon	ham sandwich
une part de pizza	slice of pizza
chauffer	to heat up
la monnaie	change

Une boulangerie

CULTURAL TIPS

If you order *un jambon beurre* in a *café*, you will be brought half a *baguette* sliced horizontally, spread with butter and filled with ham.

Other traditional French breads are:
– *une flûte*, the same length as a *baguette* but wider and weighing 400g. It is called *un pain* in Paris.
– *une ficelle,* thinner and confusingly called *une flûte* in some regions of France.
– *un bâtard*, the same width as *une flûte* but the same weight as a *baguette*.
– *une tresse*, when the dough is braided.
– *un pain de campagne*, a farmhouse loaf which is larger, heavier and coarser in texture.

Some towns in France have a particular type of bread, such as *le pain de Beaucaire* and *la couronne bordelaise. Une fougasse*, a flat bread with olives, cheese or other ingredients added, is found throughout Provence.

The traditional *boulangerie* will proudly indicate that it is a *boulangerie artisanale,* where the *boulanger* makes and cooks his own bread on site. He chooses his ingredients, kneads and lets his dough ferment and no element is ever frozen. His status is protected by law, which means that other places where bread can be purchased, including supermarkets, can only be called bread outlets.

With more than 33,000 *boulangeries artisanales* serving more than 10 million clients daily, France is the only developed country to have maintained such an important network of traditional breadmaking. This is a good reason to push open the door of a *boulangerie* while in France and proof that the stereotype of the Frenchman on a bike with a *baguette* under his arm still has some truth in it.

FRANCE IS THE ONLY DEVELOPED COUNTRY TO HAVE MAINTAINED SUCH AN IMPORTANT NETWORK OF TRADITIONAL BREADMAKING.

🔊 IDIOMS

There are lots of idioms related to bread, demonstrating again its importance for the French.

– *Avoir du pain sur la planche* means to have a lot on one's plate.
– *Long comme un jour sans pain* means interminable.
– *Il est bon comme du bon pain* means someone is extremely kind-hearted.
– *Je ne mange pas de ce pain-là* means I'm not getting involved in that.
– *Acheter quelque chose pour une bouchée de pain* is to buy something for a song, or inexpensively.

Une boulangerie

HISTORY AND TRADITIONS

Being a *boulanger* in France was initially a dangerous trade and early *boulangeries* had barred windows to prevent angry crowds from attacking them as they were considered to be charging excessively high prices. It was only in the early 19th century, as crop failures and famine became less common, and notably with the opening of the Zang Boulangerie bringing the Austrian tradition of *les petits pains viennois* to Paris, that *boulangeries* began to change. By the mid-19th century they had become highly decorated shops, with engraved windows and marble counters. *Boulangeries* soon opened in rural areas also and improved techniques lead to the flowering of the French breadmaking tradition in the mid-20th century. The French *baguette* became reputed worldwide, and by the end of the century numerous special and regional breads were also being made.

In rural areas, the evening meal traditionally consisted of soup with bread in it. How well certain breads absorbed the moisture without losing their texture was a serious topic of conversation.

In 1995, with competition from large industrialised bakers growing, a law was passed to ensure that only when the complete breadmaking process was carried out at the place of sale could the word *boulangerie* be used.

French people used to go out two or three times a day to buy a fresh loaf for each meal. This was mainly because a *baguette* quickly becomes hard, but also because people had memories of the war, when bread was rationed and often eaten stale, so being able to shop for fresh bread was a sign of improved times. Nowadays, a busy lifestyle means that most French people purchase their bread once a day.

🔊 USEFUL PHRASES

– Je voudrais une baguette bien cuite, s'il vous plaît.
I'd like a nice, crisp baguette, please.
– Je préfère pas trop cuite, s'il vous plaît.
Not too crisp for me, please.
– Vous pouvez me le trancher, s'il vous plaît ?
Can you slice it for me, please?
– Vous pouvez ne me donner que la moitié, s'il vous plaît ?
Can you give me just half a loaf, please?
– Je prendrai deux parts de pizza, s'il vous plaît.
I'll have two slices of pizza, please.
– Je voudrais une quiche aux poireaux, s'il vous plaît.
I'd like a leek quiche, please.
– Deux pains au chocolat, s'il vous plaît.
Two chocolate-filled pastries, please.
– Vous avez un pain complet ?
Do you have a wholemeal/whole wheat loaf?

Une boulangerie

CULTURAL TIPS

French loaves which have an elongated form are often given to the customer with a small piece of paper taped around the middle of the loaf so it can be held without getting flour on the hands.

Boulangeries artisanales open early, about seven in the morning, and close at lunchtime. In the afternoons, they open between three and four o'clock until seven or seven thirty in the evening. On Sundays they are open only in the mornings. *Boulangeries* close one day a week and those located in the same district will choose a different weekday from each other.

Croissants are as famous worldwide as the *baguette*. Served fresh for breakfast, they are often considered as a treat on Sunday mornings. The most popular type of *croissant*, the *croissant au beurre*, is straight and doesn't have the traditional form of a *croissant,* which is reserved for the *croissant ordinaire*, made with margarine. A good *boulanger* will pay special attention to the quality of his *croissants* and there are many national and regional competitions to find the best *croissant*.

🔊 LANGUAGE TIPS

A *baguette* can have other meanings in French. *Une baguette magique* is a magic wand, and if you eat a Chinese meal you will use *des baguettes* rather than a knife and fork.

Before going into a *boulangerie*, it's a good idea to prepare what you want to say. This means that you won't have to answer so many questions and your task will be simpler. If you want to buy a wholemeal loaf and have it sliced, you can ask for:
– *Un pain complet en tranches, s'il vous plaît.*

When you go into a *boulangerie*, remember to greet the salesperson by saying '*bonjour, madame*', or just '*bonjour*', if the person is young. As you leave they will almost certainly say:
– *Passez une bonne journée.*
To which you can reply:
– *Merci, vous aussi.*

🔊 YOU WILL HEAR

– *C'est à qui le tour ?*
  Who's next?
– *Vous aimez bien cuit ou pas trop ?*
  Do you like it crisp or not?
– *Vous le voulez en tranches ?*
  Would you like it sliced?
– *Désolée, il n'en reste plus.*
  I'm sorry, I don't have any left.
– *Il ne me reste que du pain complet ou des baguettes.*
  I've only got wholemeal/whole wheat loaves or French sticks left.
– *Vous voulez que je vous chauffe la quiche ?*
  Do you want me to heat up the quiche?
– *Vous avez de la monnaie ?*
  Do you have any change?
– *J'aurai une autre fournée dans une heure.*
  I'll have a fresh batch in an hour.
– *Il vous faut autre chose ?*
  Do you need anything else?

Une boulangerie

🔊 *Remember*

If you are in France on the 16th of May, you will see *boulangers* celebrating the feast day of Saint-Honoré, their patron saint.

At a family meal, a *baguette* is usually broken with the hands rather than cut with a knife. Each piece is then placed directly on the table, not on a plate.

Wiping a plate with a piece of bread to enjoy the last traces of a sauce is commonly practised, although in polite society the piece of bread will be placed on the prongs of a fork.

In a restaurant, any bread uneaten at the end of the main dish will be left on the table to be eaten with the cheese course. The crumbs and the bread will be cleared before the dessert is served.

🔊 ADVANCED USEFUL PHRASES

– *Je pense que c'est à moi.*
  I think it's my turn.
– *J'aimerais commander trois pains de campagne pour demain, s'il vous plaît.*
  I'd like to order three farmhouse loaves for tomorrow, please.
– *Vous pouvez me couper un morceau de votre pain aux noix, s'il vous plaît ?*
  Could you cut me a piece of your walnut loaf, please?
– *Vous avez quelles sortes de pizza ?*
  What kind of pizza do you have?
– *Qu'est-ce que vous avez comme viennoiseries ?*
  What pastries do you have?
– *Vous pouvez me mettre deux baguettes de côté, s'il vous plaît ? Je passerai les prendre tout à l'heure.*
  Can you keep two French sticks for me, please? I'll come back for them later.

 LEARN MORE

You can find examples of asking for different cakes in *Une pâtisserie chocolaterie*, p.45.

For more examples of phrases you can use when paying, you can refer to *Un restaurant*, p.22.

Une boulangerie

Most famous

The first luxury French *boulangerie* was, in fact, opened by an Austrian, August Zang, in Paris in 1838.

Among well-known *boulangeries* today are the Boulangeries Paul, which can be found throughout France and even in other countries. They use traditional bread-making techniques in their bakeries and are reputed for the quality of their bread.

Every city in France will have one, or several, famous *boulangeries*. In Paris there are notably:
– Au Levain d'Antan
– Boulangerie Bazin
– Gontran Cherrier

And the winner of the annual *Grand prix de la baguette de la ville de Paris* serves bread for a year to the Élysée Palace, the official residence of the French president.

KEY POINTS

Boulangeries...

- sell bread, *viennoiseries*, pizzas and quiches and sometimes cakes.
- close one day a week.
- offer a choice of traditional breads.
- will cut a loaf into slices at your request.
- will allow you to choose whether you want a loaf that is crisp or less well-baked.

Quiz

Choose the correct answer.

1. **Artisan *boulangers* are required by law to:**
    a) sell cakes as well as bread.
    b) wrap the bread in paper.
    c) make the bread on the premises.

2. **A *croissant au beurre* is:**
    a) straight.
    b) cresent shaped.
    c) round.

3. **When you press a *baguette* it should:**
    a) leave a dent.
    b) spring back into shape.
    c) crumble.

4. **In polite society, when you wipe your plate with a piece of bread, you should use:**
    a) your left hand.
    b) a fork.
    c) a large piece of bread.

Answers: 1. c, 2. a, 3. b, 4. b

Une pâtisserie chocolaterie

WHAT TO EXPECT

Pastel-coloured macaroons, intriguing concoctions filled with confectioner's cream, fruit piled on small round tarts, tempting chocolate cakes in all shapes and sizes; the cakes in the window of a *pâtisserie* in France catch the eye of every passer-by. You cannot help but stop and admire the variety of colourful, enticing rows of small cakes promising so much pleasure.

Once inside the shop, the larger cakes and tarts rival for attention. It's a difficult choice. That multi-layered sponge and cream cake? Or maybe that frozen dessert in its revolving showcase?

The tart with its seasonal fresh fruit looks particularly attractive, but so does that intriguing square chocolate cake labelled *un opéra*, its name adding to its appeal.

Of course, you have yet to look at the shelves devoted to chocolates. Choose a box and have it filled with chocolates: dark chocolates with rich, creamy fillings, long chocolate strips containing bitter orange peel, milk chocolates with delicate-tasting centres and mysterious dark chocolates glittering with gold leaf.

CULTURAL TIPS

If you are invited to a French person's house for a meal, you can offer to bring the dessert from a *pâtisserie chocolaterie*. This is a way of limiting the amount of work for your hostess and is generally much appreciated. Remember however to inform your hostess of your intention in advance!

When choosing a gift for French friends, chocolates are a good idea. The price for each size of box, or *ballotin,* is shown so, depending on how much you want to pay, you can choose the size of box and then have it filled with your choice of chocolates.

Une pâtisserie chocolaterie

When buying chocolates for the end-of-year holiday season, you may find long queues in high-quality *chocolateries*. French people like to have chocolates to give visitors and as gifts. Many French companies also order chocolates for employees and clients. This time of year is therefore particularly busy for these shops, as is Easter.

Among the traditional cakes to be found in a *pâtisserie* are the amusingly named *les puits d'amour*, literally wells of love, *le Paris Brest*, which sounds like a train but is in fact a choux pastry ring filled with praline-flavoured cream and *une religieuse*, an iced cream puff in a shape reminiscent of a nun.

It's a remarkable display and the result of many hours of delicate, skilful work. Like a top chef, the creations of the *pâtissier chocolatier* must not only please the eye but also have a taste and texture that will make customers want to come back for more. Innovation is as important as the capacity to produce impeccable examples of traditional cakes and chocolates.

Many *pâtissiers* and *chocolatiers* will have honed their skills working with some of the great names of the profession. All will have spent years in training and some, even when they are established, will

> INNOVATION IS AS IMPORTANT AS THE CAPACITY TO PRODUCE IMPECCABLE EXAMPLES OF TRADITIONAL CAKES AND CHOCOLATES.

◀)) KEYWORDS

une vitrine	shop window
un gâteau	cake
une tarte aux pommes	apple tart
un mille-feuille	vanilla cream slice
un macaron	macaroon
une bûche de Noël	Yule log
fourré à la crème	filled with cream
à base de génoise	sponge-based (cake)
un dessert glacé	frozen dessert
un ballotin	a small box (for chocolates)
un sachet	bag
le chocolat au lait	milk chocolate
le chocolat noir	dark chocolate
le chocolat blanc	white chocolate
un œuf de Pâques	Easter egg
une sélection	selection
choisir	to choose
offrir	to give (a present)

Une pâtisserie chocolaterie

have spent months or even years competing for the prestigious title of *Meilleur Ouvrier de France*, a title confirming that they are at the top of their profession and symbolised by narrow bands of blue, white and red around the base of their chef's collars.

In a *pâtisserie chocolaterie*, the eye-catching displays will vary with the seasons: in December, decorated *bûches* or Yule logs, a traditional French Christmas dessert; glazed *galettes des Rois* with their cardboard crowns for Twelfth Night; bell-shaped Easter chocolates and fresh fruit tarts throughout the summer months.

Regional specialities will also have their place: *les calissons d'Aix-en-Provence*, *les coussins de Lyon*, *le far breton*, *le gâteau nantais*, to name just a few. Attractively packaged, they will make perfect gifts or souvenirs of a particular town or region.

To add to the experience, some *pâtisseries chocolateries* will have a few tables so that you can choose and enjoy a cake on the spot, along with a refreshing cup of tea. However pleasurable it is to look at the enticing shop window displays, tasting is definitely to be recommended!

🔊 IDIOMS

– *Être chocolat* means to be frustrated or thwarted.
– *Ce n'est pas de la tarte* means it's no picnic.
– *C'est un papa gâteau* means he's a real softie of a dad.
– *C'est du gâteau* means it's a piece of cake.
– *C'est la cerise sur le gâteau* means it's the icing on the cake.

Une pâtisserie chocolaterie

HISTORY AND TRADITIONS

Catherine de Medicis brought the practice of eating something sweet at the end of a meal from Italy. The word dessert comes from the French *desservir,* meaning to clear the table, after which sweet delicacies were brought for guests. It was considered a sign of wealth that the table could be reset, and the word desserts came to refer to the sweet dishes themselves. Initially only the aristocracy served desserts and this remained true until the 19th century.

When chocolate was introduced to France in the 17th century, chefs began to include chocolate in desserts too and François Massialot invented *la crème au chocolat*. In 1730, Nicolas Stohrer left Versailles and opened a *pâtisserie* in Paris. It is still a renowned *pâtisserie* today.

At the court of Louis XIV, desserts were rich and elaborate. Great *pâtissiers* such as Vatel and Antonin Carême designed complicated, architectural-like structures. But when Carême also introduced the measuring of exact quantities, he took the first step towards creating recipes that could be copied by others.

CULTURAL TIPS

In France, Easter is associated with bell-shaped chocolates. The church bells are silenced from the Thursday before Easter as a sign of mourning. It is said they have gone to Rome. On their return they bring back chocolate eggs and bells, which they drop in gardens for children to find.

La galettes des Rois is a round, flat cake with marzipan filling eaten on Twelfth Night. Traditionally, the youngest child present hides under the table and decides which person receives each slice. Hidden inside the cake is a small charm and the person who finds it wears the cardboard crown given with the cake for the rest of the meal.

Les madeleines de Commercy, small oval sponge cakes, are, of course, the cakes that triggered the flood of childhood memories for Proust when he ate one dipped in a cup of tea. The famous French writer recounts the incident in the first novel of À LA RECHERCHE DU TEMPS PERDU, one of the great classics of French literature.

🔊 USEFUL PHRASES

— *Je prendrai la grande tarte aux fruits, s'il vous plaît.*
I'll take the large fruit tart, please.
— *Je voudrais quatre gâteaux individuels, s'il vous plaît.*
I would like four small cakes, please.
— *Je préfère un dessert glacé, s'il vous plaît.*
I prefer a frozen dessert, please.
— *Avez-vous des mille-feuilles ?*
Do you have any vanilla cream slices?
— *Je voudrais un ballotin de 500g, s'il vous plaît.*
I'd like a 500g box of chocolates, please.
— *Vous pouvez me mettre une sélection, s'il vous plaît ?*
Can you give me a selection, please?
— *Je préfère le chocolat noir.*
I prefer dark chocolate.
— *Vous pouvez me faire un paquet-cadeau, s'il vous plaît ?*
Can you giftwrap it for me, please?

Une pâtisserie chocolaterie

A tradition of classical French desserts evolved and in 1825 the famous epicurean Brillat-Savarin wrote about numerous cakes, many of which are still eaten today. By the end of the 19th century, French *pâtisserie* was flourishing.

The 20th century saw a move toward industrialisation as it became possible to control oven temperatures precisely. This and two world wars, with strict rationing and no butter, led to a huge decline in the number of *pâtisseries*. However, later in the century great *pâtissiers* such as Gaston Lenôtre and Pierre Hermé brought new impetus to the profession. Today, French *pâtisseries* and chocolates have a worldwide reputation.

 **Remember**

When buying cakes, if there is an ingredient you wish to avoid, you can say:
– *Je voudrais un gâteau sans chocolat, s'il vous plaît.*
I want a cake without chocolate, please.

Most *pâtisseries chocolateries* will also sell a small selection of sweets or *confiseries*, in particular *les pâtes de fruit* are usually on sale. These are squares of jellied fruit sprinkled with sugar and they are sold by weight. Be careful, they are quite heavy! There may also be small bags of them available for sale so you will be able to see how many there are for a given price.

YOU WILL HEAR

– *Je peux vous proposer une tarte aux abricots ou aux cerises ?*
I've got apricot or cherry tart.
– *Vous voulez la grande tarte ou la petite ?*
Do you want the large or the small tart?
– *Je n'ai plus de macarons. Je suis désolée.*
I have no macaroons left. I'm sorry.
– *C'est à base de génoise avec une crème pâtissière.*
It's a sponge with confectioner's custard.
– *Vous avez une préférence ?*
Do you have a preference?
– *Je vous fais un mélange ?*
Shall I give you a mixture?
– *Ça vous va comme ça ?*
Is that about right?
– *C'est pour offrir ?*
Would you like it giftwrapped?

Une pâtisserie chocolaterie

🔊 LANGUAGE TIPS

When choosing a tart, you will often be asked how many people you want to serve. It may be easier to include this information in your initial request. You can say:
– *Je voudrais une tarte aux pommes pour huit personnes, s'il vous plaît.*
I'd like an apple tart for eight people, please.

When you don't know the name of a cake you would like to buy, you can indicate your choice by describing an element of the cake. You might say:
– *Je voudrais le gâteau avec le dessus en chocolat, s'il vous plaît.*
I'd like the cake with chocolate on top, please.
– *C'est celui derrière le gâteau au chocolat et à côté de la tarte aux pommes.*
It's the one behind the chocolate cake and next to the apple tart.

🔊 ADVANCED USEFUL PHRASES

– *Qu'est-ce qu'il y a à l'intérieur ?*
What's inside?
– *Comment ce gâteau s'appelle-t-il?*
What's this cake called?
– *Vous pouvez me faire une petite sélection en privilégiant les chocolats noirs, s'il vous plaît ?*
Can you give me a selection with mainly dark chocolates, please?
– *C'est une spécialité régionale ? Qu'est-ce que c'est exactement ?*
Is it a regional speciality? What is it exactly?
– *Je voudrais faire un petit cadeau à quelqu'un. Vous pouvez me suggérer quelque chose ?*
I want to give a present to someone. Can you suggest something?
– *Combien de temps faut-il le sortir du frigo avant de le manger ?*
How long do I need to take it out of the fridge before eating it?
– *C'est suffisamment grand pour six personnes ?*
Is it big enough for six people?
– *Vous avez une tarte avec plusieurs fruits différents ?*
Do you have a tart with several different fruits?

 **LEARN MORE**

You can find more examples of identifying what you want when you don't know the exact name in *Une fromagerie*, p.52.

For further examples of specifying quantities, you can refer to *Le marché*, p.68.

Une pâtisserie chocolaterie

Most famous

Incredibly, France's oldest *pâtisserie*, which opened in Paris in 1730, is still open today. Although the original building no longer stands, it is in a listed 19th century building at the same address, 51 rue Montorgueil in the 2nd *arrondissement*. Among the specialities of the *pâtisserie* is the famous *Baba au rhum* first created by Nicolas Stohrer for King Stanislas of Poland.

Arnaud Larher, *maître patissier et chocolatier*, has three shops in the Montmartre district of Paris. He is one of France's top talents and was recognised as a *Meilleur Ouvrier de France* in 2007.

Gaston Lenôtre, considered by many to be the greatest *pâtissier* ever, died in 2009, but the business he created has shops in Paris and throughout France as well as in many other countries.

Lovers of chocolate will want to visit La Maison du chocolat. The first boutique was opened in the rue du Faubourg Saint-Honoré in Paris in 1977. There are now boutiques in New York, London and Tokyo.

Quiz

Match the first half of the sentence with its second half.

A. *Je prendrai un ballotin...*

B. *Est-ce que vous avez...*

C. *Il me faut une tarte...*

D. *C'est le gâteau derrière...*

E. *Je prendrai la galette...*

F. *Qu'est-ce que vous avez comme...*

1. *pour six personnes, s'il vous plaît.*

2. *la tarte aux abricots.*

3. *de cinq cents grammes, s'il vous plaît.*

4. *un dessert glacé ?*

5. *bûches de Noël ?*

6. *des Rois, s'il vous plaît.*

Answers: A3, B4, C1, D2, E6, F5.

KEY POINTS

Pâtisseries chocolateries...

● have attractive window displays.
● let you choose the chocolates you want to include in a box.
● are open on Sunday mornings but close one day a week.
● sell regional specialities that make good gifts.
● are very busy at Easter and the end of the year.

Une fromagerie

WHAT TO EXPECT

You can eat a different French cheese every day of the year. In fact, that is an understatement. France has more than 400 cheeses and the French eat an average of 24 kilos per person each year. No wonder then that entering a *fromagerie* is such a journey of discovery.

First, there is the smell. Forget the old myth that all French cheeses smell bad. *Fromageries* smell wonderful and have a variety of different odours. Then, there is the display: cheeses of all shapes and sizes and different textures. You can play it safe and choose a cheese you recognise or be bold and let yourself be tempted by cheeses you didn't even know existed.

CULTURAL TIPS

A *fromagerie* is often called a *fromagerie-crémerie* as it will usually sell dairy products such as milk and eggs as well.

Have you ever wondered why a French person will open a box of French Camembert and press the contents with the thumb? This is a way of testing the cheese to see how ripe it is. The softer to the touch, the riper the Camembert.

In France, cheese is served before, not after, the dessert and is accompanied by bread rather than crackers. You can use any bread left over after your main course, which will have been left on the table by your hostess or waiter, and then take a fresh piece if you need more.

ENTERING A *FROMAGERIE* IS A JOURNEY OF DISCOVERY.

Une fromagerie

Luckily you can rely on the *fromager* or his or her assistants for guidance. They will point out which cheeses are made from cow's milk, which from goat's milk and which from ewe's milk. Then there are the different categories: *les pâtes molles*, or soft cheeses, *les pâtes dures* or *pressées*, hard or pressed cheeses, and cheeses *à pâte persillée*, which are blue cheeses. Finally, some cheeses are more or less ripe depending on the type and length of the maturing process.

An enthusiastic *fromager* will not only give you a virtual tour of the French regions, but also provide many insights into the cheese-making process. A *fromager* does not only buy cheeses from different producers and then resell them, in some cases he will carry out the maturing process himself and he will be an expert at knowing just when a cheese is at its peak.

🔊 KEYWORDS

un morceau	piece
une tranche	slice
un peu de	a bit of
le goût	taste
l'odeur	smell
fait	ripe
pas trop fait	not too ripe
crémeux	creamy
coulant	runny
un fromage de vache	cow's milk cheese
un fromage de chèvre	goat's milk cheese
un fromage de brebis	ewe's milk cheese
un fromage bleu	blue cheese
râpé	grated
la croûte	rind
l'affinage	maturing
le lait cru	unpasteurised milk
le prix	price
la caisse	cash desk

Une fromagerie

CULTURAL TIPS

When a selection of cheese is offered during a meal and you wish to take a piece from a cheese which has a pointed shape, such as a piece of Brie, or is thinner at one edge, such as a Roquefort, make sure you don't cut off the point or just take the thinner edge. It is frowned upon to have *coupé le nez au fromage*, or cut the nose of the cheese. Just cut a piece down the side of the cheese to show your *savoir-faire*.

If you take a selection of two or three cheeses, you should eat the milder-tasting cheeses first and leave the stronger cheeses, such as blue cheeses, until the end so as to fully appreciate each cheese.

In a *fromagerie*, you may see little plastic pots, often with holes down the sides. They contain *fromage blanc*, which is a creamy product made from drained milk curds and usually eaten with sugar and topped with cream.

🔊 IDIOMS

– *Il en a fait tout un fromage* means he made a big fuss about it.
– *Entre la poire et le fromage* means casually or light-heartedly.
– *Trouver un bon fromage* means to find a cushy job.
– *Changer de crémerie* means to go elsewhere.

You can inquire about the specialities of the area you are visiting while also discovering the cheeses of other areas of France. Choose a creamy Camembert from Normandy, a bleu-veined Roquefort from the valleys of Aveyron, a firm Beaufort from the hills of the Jura or a small round goat's cheese from the Ardèche, just to name a few.

Once you have made your choice, you will be asked what quantity you require. For hard cheeses and blue cheeses, the *fromager* will place his knife to indicate a larger- or smaller-sized wedge. Don't be afraid to ask for the knife to be moved to give the thickness you require. Soft cheeses will usually be sold as circular, square or log-shaped units depending on the type of cheese.

When you are ready to pay you may be a little surprised. Good cheese is expensive. But the final pleasure is still to come: tasting that newly discovered French cheese with a freshly baked *baguette*.

Une fromagerie

HISTORY AND TRADITIONS

As early as the first century, the Romans were already singing the praises of French cheeses. Later, Benedictine and Cistercian monks, for whom cheese was a staple food, were responsible for inventing ripening techniques and a huge increase in cheese-making followed.

In the Middle Ages, peasants suffering from famine also started producing cheese as a way of conserving milk as long as possible, and gradually the various cheeses became known by the name of the regions in which they were produced. It was only in the late 18th century that the wealthy classes began eating cheese, and the practice of a selection of cheeses being served towards the end of a meal only became common in the 19th century.

THE VARIOUS CHEESES BECAME KNOWN BY THE NAME OF THE REGIONS IN WHICH THEY WERE PRODUCED.

🔊 USEFUL PHRASES

– *Je voudrais un camembert, s'il vous plaît.*
  A Camembert, please.
– *Un morceau de brie, s'il vous plaît.*
  A piece of Brie, please.
– *C'est un fromage de vache ?*
  Is it made from cow's milk?
– *Je prendrai quatre fromages blancs, s'il vous plaît.*
  I'll take four fromage blancs, please.
– *Ça vient de quelle région ?*
  Which region does it come from?
– *Ça a un goût très fort ?*
  Does it have a very strong taste?
– *Je voudrais juste un petit morceau, s'il vous plaît.*
  I just want a small piece, please.
– *Ça me fait trop. Un morceau plus petit, s'il vous plaît.*
  That's too much. A smaller piece, please.

Une fromagerie

Smelly cheeses – and there are several – are not necessarily the strongest tasting.

Fromageries are usually open from about half past eight until midday and then again in the afternoon until about seven. They will also be open on Sunday mornings. They close one day a week, often on Mondays.

Some French cheeses are made from unpasteurised milk, *au lait cru*, but this will be indicated on the label or mentioned when you inquire about them.

If you don't want to shock your French guests, make sure you don't serve cheese directly from the fridge. Keep it in a cool place; a cellar is perfect. If you have no alternative but the fridge, make sure you take it out in advance, but don't leave it somewhere very warm or any creamy cheeses will become very runny.

As cheeses began to be transported by rail, scientific techniques were introduced to increase conservation, and with the discovery of pasteurisation, one of the first industrialised cheese manufacturing processes was estalished by Léon Bel in the east of France. The famous *La vache qui rit* cheese, now a global brand, was created there in 1921.

In order to protect the distinctive nature of traditional regional cheeses and their characteristic methods of production, some cheeses have been accorded an AOC *(Appellation d'origine contrôlée)*, a label of origin. Roquefort cheese, first made in the ninth century, was the first French cheese to receive an AOC in 1925. Today, there are more than 40 AOC cheeses.

For the French, the huge variety and quality of French cheese is an important part of their cultural heritage. You can start to appreciate how true this is by entering a *fromagerie*.

🔊 YOU WILL HEAR

— *Qu'est-ce que vous désirez ?*
   What would you like?
— *Oui, c'est un fromage de la région.*
   Yes, it's a local cheese.
— *Vous préférez bien fait ou pas ?*
   Do you prefer it very ripe or not?
— *C'est un fromage de chèvre fait en Ardèche.*
   It's a goat's cheese from the Ardèche.
— *Je vous coupe un morceau ?*
   Shall I cut a piece for you?
— *Vous en voulez un morceau comme ça ou moins ?*
   Do you want a piece like this or smaller?
— *Il vous fallait autre chose ?*
   Do you require anything else?
— *Alors, je vous mets tout ça dans un sac.*
   I'll put all that in a bag for you then.

Une fromagerie

🔊 LANGUAGE TIPS

If you're not sure of the names of cheeses, you can ask for them by pointing. However, as there are likely to be a lot of different cheeses close together, you will need to be precise. You can say:
– *Le deuxième à gauche.*
The second on the left.
– *Non, celui qui est derrière.*
No, the one behind it.
– *Celui qui est juste devant.*
The one that's just in front.
– *Non, celui qui est juste à côté.*
No, the one just next to it.

In the case of hard cheeses, the *fromager* may cut a little piece for you to taste. He will say:
– *Tenez. Goûtez.*
Here you are. Try it.

🔊 *Remember*

In a *fromagerie*, if you prefer cheese that is not too ripe, you can specify this by saying:
– *Pas trop fait, s'il vous plaît.*
Not too ripe, please.

Fromageries will stock a huge variety of cheeses and not even French people will recognise every one, so don't be afraid to ask for help in identifying them.

If you don't want cheese during a meal, you can simply say:
– *Pas de fromage pour moi, merci.*
No cheese for me, thanks.

Un fruitier is a person who makes cheese and *une fruitière* is the place where cheese is made, whereas *une fromagerie* is the place where cheese is sold.

🔊 ADVANCED USEFUL PHRASES

– *Je voudrais un camembert pas trop fait, s'il vous plaît.*
I'd like a Camembert that is not too ripe, please.
– *C'est fait à partir de lait cru ?*
Is it made from unpasteurised milk?
– *C'est un fromage qui a été affiné longtemps ?*
Is it a cheese that has been matured for a long time?
– *J'aime bien les fromages forts. Qu'est-ce que vous pouvez me recommander ?*
I like strong cheese. What can you recommend?
– *Vous avez plusieurs sortes de comté. Quelle est la différence entre eux ?*
You have several kinds of Comté. What is the difference between them?
– *D'où viennent ces différentes fromages bleus ?*
Where do these various blue cheeses come from?
– *Ce morceau-là est trop petit. Il me faut un morceau plus grand.*
That piece is too small. I need a bigger piece.
– *Il faut payer à la caisse ?*
Do I pay at the cash desk?

🐦 LEARN MORE

You can find more information on eating cheese in *Un restaurant*, p.22.

For other examples of buying food, you can refer to *Le marché*, p.68.

Une fromagerie

Most famous

The cheeses from the Fromagerie Delin, based in the Côte-d'Or, can be found in Dijon's market hall. *Fromagers* for four generations, their cheeses have won many prizes.

Not far away in Beaune, Alain Hess, creator of the *Délice de Pommard*, is an established *fromager* who supplies the highly-reputed restaurants of the region. His *fromagerie* in the town centre is known for its old-world charm as well as the quality of its cheeses.

The Androuet Mouffetard *fromagerie* in the 5th *arrondissement* in Paris was established in 1909. You can find more than 250 cheeses made from unpasteurised milk and matured on the premises, as well as many others. There are several linked *fromageries* also in Paris, and all are highly reputed. Androuet Verneuil in the 7th *arrondissement* is a long-established *fromagerie*, as is Androuet Terasse in the 17th *arrondissement*.

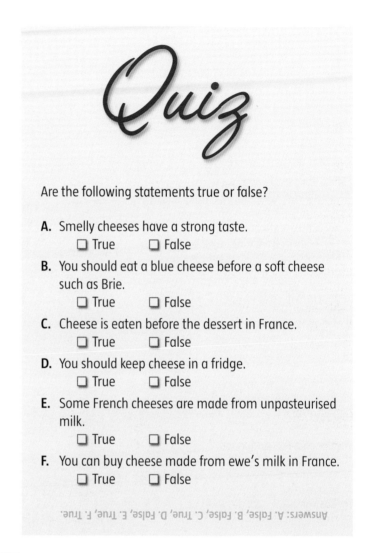

Quiz

Are the following statements true or false?

A. Smelly cheeses have a strong taste.
☐ True   ☐ False

B. You should eat a blue cheese before a soft cheese such as Brie.
☐ True   ☐ False

C. Cheese is eaten before the dessert in France.
☐ True   ☐ False

D. You should keep cheese in a fridge.
☐ True   ☐ False

E. Some French cheeses are made from unpasteurised milk.
☐ True   ☐ False

F. You can buy cheese made from ewe's milk in France.
☐ True   ☐ False

Answers: A. False, B. False, C. True, D. False, E. True, F. True.

KEY POINTS

Fromageries...

- sell a large variety of cheeses from the different regions of France.
- will have a selection of local cheeses.
- usually sell milk and eggs too.
- are open on Sunday mornings but close one day a week.
- will have assistants able to explain the different cheeses on display.

Une charcuterie traiteur

WHAT TO EXPECT

Savour a slice of *saucisson sec* as you drink your *apéritif*. Bite into a *baguette* filled with ham and butter on a picnic. Enjoy a slice of pâté as a starter. The essential ingredients can all be bought at the local *charcuterie*.

The main street of every French town will have at least one, and probably several, *charcuteries*. These shops traditionally sell food products made from pork, so when you go in, you will see enticing displays of sausages, salami, hams, black puddings and lots of pâtés. Various knives and machines allow the *charcutier* to serve wafer-thin slices of salted raw ham or thick wedges of crusted pâtés. The choice is yours.

Most *charcuteries* are also *traiteurs* or caterers, so you will see lots of attractive prepared dishes, too, ranging from simple grated carrots with a French dressing to *coq au vin*. Every day, different dishes are presented to tempt those who want to take some time off from cooking. Some *charcuteries* will have particular dishes on sale on a specific day of the week so that customers who have particular favourites know when to come by. Many French people, however, just walk in knowing that there will always be something to delight them.

CULTURAL TIPS

When French people are preparing a picnic, they will often buy a *saucisson*, a dry sausage. This is so commonly associated with picnics that the word *saucissoner* has come to mean to have a picnic or to eat a snack.

Le boudin blanc is a white sausage filled with a mixture of minced white meat, milk and bread. Unlike *le boudin*, there is no blood in it. Other ingredients such as truffles can be added and most *charcutiers* will have their own recipe. *Le boudin blanc* is particularly present in *charcuteries* around the end-of-year holiday period. It is usually fried gently in butter until the skin becomes golden.

Une charcuterie traiteur

On a Sunday morning or on a holiday, and even on Christmas morning, don't be surprised if you see people waiting outside the local *charcuterie traiteur*. The French often order special dishes when they have large gatherings of family and friends. On Christmas morning, you will see people emerging from a *charcuterie traiteur* with large presentation dishes of salmon, cold meats or lobster. Having stopped by a few days previously to choose a festive dish from a list prepared by the *charcutier*, customers pick up their order, freshly prepared, on Christmas morning itself.

CULTURAL TIPS

If you go to a wine tasting or into a wine bar, you will probably be served slices of *saucisson sec* with your glass of wine. While the *saucisson* goes well with the wine, the practice may be linked to the nature of the proprietor's licence and the laws for selling alcohol. Most licences only allow the sale and consumption of alcohol on site if it is accompanied by food. A few slices of *saucisson* can help avoid problems.

When buying portions of ready-cooked dishes, the *charcuterie traiteur* will show you differently sized containers, *des barquettes*, so you can decide on the quantities you require. These are then usually sealed so that they are easy to carry.

You will find many elaborately prepared cold dishes, too, in a *charcuterie traiteur*. These will be particularly varied around holiday periods. Sometimes French hostesses will order one of these dishes, such as a fish terrine or dressed lobster, to serve as starters when they have guests. It helps to limit the preparation time needed when entertaining in the evening.

THE DISPLAYS IN A
CHARCUTERIE TRAITEUR
CHANGE WITH THE SEASONS.

🔊 IDIOMS

— If somebody talks about kids in a familiar way, they may refer to them as *les lardons*, literally diced bacon fat.
— Referring to a girl as *un boudin* is not very flattering. It means she's a fat lump.
— *Ne pas attacher son chien avec des saucisses* means to be tight with money.

Une charcuterie traiteur

The displays in a *charcuterie traiteur* change with the seasons. In the autumn there will be cooked game dishes, in summer, fish or vegetable terrines and around the New Year you can try *boudin blanc*, a white pudding. Each region has its traditional specialities. You will be surprised at how much salami-style sausages can vary in different parts of France. Of course, every *charcutier* will maintain that the local variety is by far the best.

Even if you don't need to buy anything, you can still enjoy the magnificent window displays. They demonstrate the importance the French give to food and its preparation. Appetising and artistically presented, the individual dishes are fascinating insights into what the French like to eat at home and order for guests.

🔊 KEYWORDS

une tranche	slice
un morceau	piece
une barquette	container
une part	portion
une terrine	terrine
un saucisson sec	cold, slicing sausage
une saucisse	sausage
une saucisse de Morteau	type of smoked sausage
un saucisson à l'ail	garlic sausage
le boudin	black pudding/blood sausage
le jambon de pays	cured ham
le jambon de Paris	boiled ham
le pâté en croûte	raised crust pâté
un pâté de foie	liver pâté
un pâté de campagne	coarse pork pâté
les rillettes	potted pork
une côte de porc	pork chop
fin(e)	thin
épais(se)	thick

Une charcuterie traiteur

HISTORY AND TRADITIONS

Salting and smoking meat – particularly pork – in order to preserve it, dates back many centuries. However in France, it was only in the 15th century that *charcutiers* were granted the right to prepare and sell cooked or salted pork. Initially, they were obliged to buy the fresh meat from butchers and they became know as the *chairs cuitiers*, literally, those who prepared cooked meat, and finally as *charcutiers*. Their trade was highly regulated and included periods when they were not allowed to do business, such as from the middle of September to Lent. However, laws passed under Louis XII finally freed them from the domination of the butchers. Many *charcutiers* became *traiteurs*, too. They sold prepared dishes and also sometimes delivered them. A trade union for *charcutiers* was established in 1881.

CULTURAL TIPS

Many *charcutiers* will hang cured hams and bunches of *saucissons secs* from the ceiling. This makes for a colourful and traditional display. Permission will generally be given if you wish to take a photograph, but make sure you ask first.

Une assiette anglaise is a selection of *charcuterie* products such as cold slices of roasted meats, *pâté en croûte*, ham and salami-type sausages served with pickled gherkins. It is often served in cafés at lunchtime and, despite its name, its origins are French.

Most *charcuteries traiteurs* will also have just a few classic desserts such as egg custards or slices of apple tart. This allows you to buy a complete meal if you wish.

🔊 USEFUL PHRASES

– *Je voudrais huit tranches de jambon cru, s'il vous plaît.*
I'd like eight slices of cured ham, please.
– *Vous pouvez me donner un morceau de boudin, s'il vous plaît ?*
Can you give me a piece of black pudding/blood sausage, please?
– *Vous avez du pâté en croûte au canard ?*
Do you have any duck crust pie?
– *Je prendrai une barquette d'endives braisées, s'il vous plaît.*
I'll take a container of braised endives, please.
– *Une petite barquette suffit. Merci.*
A small container will do. Thank you.
– *Trois côtes de porc, s'il vous plaît.*
Three pork chops, please.
– *Vous avez un saucisson pas trop sec, s'il vous plaît ?*
Do you have a cold, slicing sausage that is not too dry, please?
– *Donnez-moi pour trois personnes, s'il vous plaît.*
Enough for three people, please.
– *C'est bon comme ça. Merci.*
That's fine like that. Thank you.
– *Ce sera tout. Merci.*
That's all. Thanks.

Une charcuterie traiteur

MAGNIFICENT WINDOW
DISPLAYS DEMONSTRATE
THE IMPORTANCE
THE FRENCH GIVE TO FOOD
AND ITS PREPARATION.

The tradition of *charcuteries traiteurs* prospered in the mid-20th century, but in recent years many businesses have closed. There are still, however, around 6,000 *charcuteries* in France.

Today, as competition from supermarket chains continues to grow, a quality label has been introduced. *Charcutiers* who prepare more than 80% of the products sold in their shops, a percentage which must include ten of the most frequently sold products such as hams and pâtés, can apply for the label. There is also a week in June when the shops and products of *charcutiers traiteurs* are celebrated. The slogan is *Mon charcutier traiteur, il a tout bon !* Both programmes aim to ensure that *charcuteries traiteurs* continue to attract customers in the main streets of French towns.

🔊 *Remember*

When in a charcuterie, you may want to spend some time looking around before making your choice. If this is the case, you can say:
– *Je prends un petit moment pour regarder, s'il vous plaît.*

If you are staying in accommodation with cooking facilities, prepared dishes from a *charcuterie traiteur* are very practical. Usually the containers used for your order are suitable for a microwave oven.

When buying cold meats such as salami-type sausages for a picnic, you can ask to have them sliced, although you will still have to remove the thin skin around each slice:
– *Vous pouvez me le trancher, s'il vous plaît?*

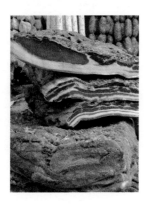

🔊 YOU WILL HEAR

– *On s'occupe de vous ?*
Are you being served?
– *Vous voulez des tranches fines ?*
Do you want thin slices?
– *Vous voulez quelle quantité ?*
How much do you want?
– *Vous voulez quelle taille de barquette ?*
What size container do you want?
– *Je vous mets un peu de sauce ?*
Shall I add some sauce?
– *Il vous fallait autre chose ?*
Do you need anything else?
– *Et avec ça ?*
Anything else?
– *Ce sera tout ?*
Will that be all?

Une charcuterie traiteur

Most famous

The Maison Hardy, situated on the Place du vieux marché in Rouen, was established in 1935. It specialises in local products including a famous *andouillette*, which was much favoured by the late Queen Mother of Great Britain.

Le Hech, on avenue du Midi in Pompadour, is famous for its *foies gras*, its *boudin aux châtaignes* and its exclusive *Tourte Pompadour*.

In Paris, the *charcuterie* Bignon – Au cochon rose, on rue Saint-Charles in the 15th *arrondissement*, has won many prizes. La Maison Pou, on avenue des Ternes in the 17th *arrondissement*, is one of the oldest *charcuteries* as it was established in 1830. Its *fromage de tête* is particularly prized. Au fin Gourmet, on rue du Faubourg-Saint-Antoine in the 12th *arrondissement*, also has a long history.

🔊 LANGUAGE TIPS

There are lots of different pâtés in a *charcuterie*: *pâté de campagne, pâté en croûte, pâté de canard, pâté de lapin*. However, if someone refers to *un pâté de maisons*, this is not something you can eat. It means a block of houses.
– *Je vais faire un tour de pâté de maisons.*
I'm going to go around the block.

But if the *charcutier* or your French hostess tells you, *"Le pâté est fait maison,"* it means it is homemade pâté and you can be sure of its quality.

When buying *pâté en croûte*, you need to say which one you want as there will probably be *pâté en croûte* made from pork, chicken, rabbit or a mixture:
– *Je prendrai deux tranches de pâté en croûte au poulet, s'il vous plaît.*
I'll take two slices of the raised-crust pâté with chicken.

🐦 **LEARN MORE**

You can find further examples of ordering quantities in the *Le marché*, p.68.

For further examples of asking for information, look in *Une crêperie, un bouchon*, p.29.

Une charcuterie traiteur

Fill in the blanks using the word bank below.
pâté, porc, morceau, barquette, tranches, côtes

A. *Je voudrais trois _____ de jambon de Paris, s'il vous plaît.*

B. *Est-ce que vous avez du _____ en croûte?*

C. *Je prendrai deux _____ de porc, s'il vous plaît.*

D. *Une _____ plus petite suffit. Merci.*

E. *Vous avez des rillettes de _____ ?*

F. *Il me faut un _____ de lard, s'il vous plaît.*

Answers: A. tranches, B. pâté, C. côtes, D. barquette, E. porc, F. morceau.

◀)) ADVANCED USEFUL PHRASES

– *Vous pouvez me couper quatre belles tranches de jambon de Paris, s'il vous plaît ?*
Can you cut four good slices of boiled ham for me, please?

– *Je préfère des tranches fines, s'il vous plaît.*
I prefer thin slices, please.

– *Il me faut deux parts de lasagne, s'il vous plaît.*
I'd like two portions of lasagne, please.

– *Mettez-m'en un peu plus, s'il vous plaît.*
I'd like a bit more, please.

– *Ça se réchauffe au micro-ondes ?*
Can I heat it in a microwave?

– *Il en faut combien pour quatre personnes, s'il vous plaît ?*
How much do I need for four people, please?

– *Qu'est-ce que vous avez comme plats à emporter ?*
What do you have for takeaway?

– *Le boudin se cuit comment ?*
How do you cook a black pudding/blood sausage?

KEY POINTS

Charcuteries traiteurs...

● sell a selection of pork-based products.
● often have a choice of ready prepared dishes.
● will take orders for dishes for festive occasions.
● have special dishes for end-of-the-year holidays.
● are open on Sunday mornings and even Christmas morning.

As they say in French

- « *Tant que l'on n'est pas un fromage, l'âge ne compte pas.* »
  Jean-Loup Chiflet

- « *Avec un saucisson à l'ail, on se sent moins seul.* »
  Paul Claudel

- « *J'apprécie plus le pain, le pâté, le saucisson que les limitations de vitesse.* »
  Jacques Chirac

- « *Si Dieu était une femme, le monde marcherait mieux. Et il y aurait moins de calories dans le chocolat et plus dans les endives.* »
  Alix Girod de l'Ain

- « *La Terre est un gâteau plein de douceur.* »
  Charles Baudelaire

Part 3

NOT TO BE MISSED

Le marché

WHAT TO EXPECT

Wandering around a French market is a colourful and enjoyable experience. It's the perfect hands-on way to learn more about the region, discover local specialities and test your ear with the local accent.

French markets come in all shapes and sizes. They may be just a few grouped stalls in a small village square, or huge markets that, on certain days, take over the main street in the town centre or a district of Paris. They may be sprawling, open-air markets in Provence, or covered markets under a historic wooden roof, or in modern purpose-built buildings. Whatever their size, each market will draw people from both the immediate area and surrounding neighbourhoods or villages. As these enthusiastic market-goers set off from home with their basket or wheeled trolley, they will announce, *"Je vais faire mon marché"*.

FRENCH MARKETS ARE THE PERFECT WAY TO LEARN MORE ABOUT THE REGION AND DISCOVER LOCAL SPECIALITIES.

CULTURAL TIPS

Be careful where you park your car in France, particularly if it's in or near a main square. Warning notices will tell you that you can park except on particular days at specific times. This is usually when the square or street is used for the market.

Stallholders will start setting up between five and six o'clock in the morning. If your hotel overlooks the village square, you may be woken up early on market day.

Le marché

Walking around a French market, you will quickly be able to distinguish between local producers *(les producteurs)* and stallholders selling a large variety of fruit and vegetables from different suppliers *(les revendeurs)*. Sometimes you will see a person, often elderly, with only a few eggs or lettuces to sell. Other stallholders will specialise in apples or endives or just potatoes and onions. Some local producers will have a selection of fruit and vegetables that vary from week to week as the seasons progress. Larger stalls with a huge variety of produce will often have products that complement the seasonal display, such as olives, dried herbs or produce from other countries. However, they will all know their products well and be able to help you choose and even give you tips as to how to prepare or cook what they sell.

Some markets will include stalls selling clothes and other goods. Some in areas frequented by tourists will have a selection of craftwork on sale. Usually there are also stalls devoted to organic produce, local honey, cheeses, fish, poultry or sausages. As you visit, you will be offered slices of *saucisson* or cheese to taste, given pieces of melon or segments of orange and encouraged to discover, compare and appreciate.

🔊 KEYWORDS

le jour du marché	market day
un marché couvert	covered market
les halles	covered market
un forain	stallholder
un étalage	stall
un plateau	metal bowl
les légumes	vegetables
les fruits	fruit
le saucisson	(salami-type) sausage
le miel	honey
le pain bio	organic bread
les fringues	clothes (slang)
le panier	basket
le cabas	shopping basket
un caddie	trolley
un cageot	crate
une livre	half a kilo
une tranche	slice
la moitié	half
une barquette	punnets/containers
mûr(e)	ripe
frais (fraîche)	fresh

Le marché

Markets have to close at a given time and stallholders must repack their produce and tables and remove their vans before this time limit. This is usually about one o'clock and ensures that the area is cleared so that the litter from the market can be removed and the area cleaned by the local services.

If you are at a market early, you may see the *placier*. This is a person employed by the local authority to check that stallholders have paid their fees and are in the right places. The *placier* also assigns any places not being used by regular stallholders to occasional stallholders.

Most stalls have metal or plastic bowls you can fill with the quantity you require of a particular fruit or vegetable. This bowl will then be weighed when your turn comes. Sometimes these bowls will be on display and filled with pears or carrots or cherries. The content may be at a special price. This can be a genuine reduction, a way of saving the client time, or a means of selling produce that is of inferior quality.

A market is an event. It often disrupts traffic, has buses timed to bring people from nearby villages on market days and in villages, small towns and even cities it will be the occasion when people meet to discuss and catch up on local gossip. Local politicians can frequently be seen shaking hands with stallholders and passers-by and the distribution of political pamphlets, particularly near election time, is common.

Near the market there will be at least one and usually several *cafés*. They open early for stallholders as they set up and later give the locals a place to sit and chat. When you have finished your tour of the market, you, too, can join the locals and watch the bustle of the market as you sip your coffee or *apéritif* in the sun.

SHOPPERS ARE ENCOURAGED TO DISCOVER, COMPARE AND APPRECIATE.

- *Faire son marché* means to do one's shopping (at the market).
- *Marché conclu !* It's a deal!
- *Par-dessus le marché* means 'on top of that'.
- *Ne pas mettre tous ses œufs dans le même panier* means not to put all one's eggs in the same basket.
- *Une grosse légume* means a bigwig or a big shot.

Le marché

HISTORY AND TRADITIONS

France has a long and dynamic tradition of markets that dates back over centuries and which has continuously flourished.

A large central market was established in Paris in 1110. A fish market and then a corn market were created on the same site in the 1st *arrondissement* and were joined by a fruit and vegetable market in 1789. Les Halles de Paris became a huge wholesale market and remained on the historic site until it was moved out of central Paris in 1969 and the site redesigned. The *quartier* is still called Les Halles today.

Every town and large village in France had its market, and in many the remarkable wooden roofs that covered the markets in medieval times can still be seen today in the central squares. Many are still in use.

In the 19th century, magnificent metallic structures were built to house the local market. Examples of these can be seen in towns such as Limoges or Dijon.

In certain regions of France the markets were dominated by local activities, such as fishing or the production of olive oil or walnuts. The markets of Provence became known for their spices and herbs and the sale of lavender.

The east of France has a long tradition of Christmas markets dating from the 16th century. These markets, with stalls selling gifts and regional products, have now spread to other regions in France. The traditional wooden cabins are set up in early December and remain throughout the holiday period. Provence also has a history of Christmas markets where you can admire the traditional nativity scenes with their humorous Provençal characters.

🔊 USEFUL PHRASES

– *Je voudrais un kilo de pommes, s'il vous plaît.*
  I'd like a pound of apples, please.
– *Une salade, s'il vous plaît, et un concombre.*
  A lettuce, please, and a cucumber.
– *Deux pêches pas trop mûres, s'il vous plaît.*
  Two peaches that aren't too ripe, please.
– *Un petit kilo de cerises, s'il vous plaît.*
  Just under a kilo of cherries, please.
– *Trois cents grammes de champignons, s'il vous plaît.*
  Three hundred grammes of mushrooms, please.
– *Une tranche de ce fromage-là, s'il vous plaît.*
  A slice of that cheese, please.
– *Je prendrai le cageot d'abricots.*
  I'll take the crate of apricots.
– *Je peux goûter ?*
  May I try it?
– *Qu'est-ce que c'est ?*
  What is it?
– *C'est tout, merci.*
  That's all, thank you.
– *Ça fait combien?*
  How much is that?

Le marché

🔊 LANGUAGE TIPS

If you don't know the name of something in French, you can point and say:
– *Je prendrai celui-là, s'il vous plaît.*
I'll take that one, please.

A pound in weight is *une livre*, whereas a book is masculine and is *un livre*.

If you're not very sure of the weight you require, you can say:
– *Il y a combien de pommes dans un kilo ?*
How many apples are there in a kilo?

Or, if you realise when the stallholder is weighing what you have asked for that you have asked for too much, you can say:
– *Vous pouvez en enlever un peu, s'il vous plaît ? Ça me fait trop.*
Can you take some off, please? That's too much for me.

🔊 YOU WILL HEAR

– *C'est à vous, Madame ?*
  Are you next?
– *Combien en voulez-vous?*
  How much/many do you want?
– *Désolé, je n'en ai plus.*
  I'm sorry, I've sold out.
– *Autre chose ?*
  Anything else?
– *Et avec ça ?*
  Do you need anything else?
– *Ça fait trop ?*
  Is that too much/many?
– *Goûtez les cerises. Elles sont très bonnes.*
  Try the cherries. They're really good.
– *Vous n'avez pas de monnaie ?*
  Do you have any change?
– *Vous avez un panier ?*
  Do you have a basket?

CULTURAL TIPS

Markets in big cities will often be smaller in summer, particularly during the month of August. In regions that attract a lot of tourists, the opposite will be true, and markets in July and August will be bigger than usual. December is a particularly busy time for markets with the build-up to the holiday period.

Most outdoor markets will be once a week, although in bigger towns they may be more frequent, sometimes nearly every day, including Saturdays and Sundays. Covered markets will usually be open at least two or three days a week.

Some products, such as prized varieties of mushrooms, will only be on sale at particular times of the year, and sometimes there will be special annual markets such as the markets for truffles, a highly valued delicacy.

Le marché

🔊 *Remember*

When you purchase fruit at a market you can request that it be more or less ripe. If you buy two melons, for example, you can say:

– *Je voudrais deux melons, un pour manger aujourd'hui et l'autre pour dimanche, s'il vous plaît.*
I want two melons, one for today and the other for Sunday, please.

In France, fish are sold and served whole with their heads. This is to show that the fish is fresh. If you are buying fish, you can ask to have it cleaned.

– *Vous pouvez me le vider, s'il vous plaît ?*
Can you clean it for me, please?

🔊 ADVANCED USEFUL PHRASES

– *C'est du fromage de brebis ?*
Is it ewe's-milk cheese?

– *Vous pouvez me couper le poulet en morceaux, s'il vous plaît?*
Can you cut the chicken into pieces, please?

– *Vous pouvez m'en mettre un peu plus ?*
Can you add a few more, please?

– *Ce sont des légumes bio?*
Are they organically grown vegetables?

– *Vous pouvez m'expliquer les différences entre ces miels, s'il vous plaît ?*
Could you explain the different varieties of honey you have, please?

– *Vous pouvez m'expliquer la différence entre ces deux saucissons ?*
Could you explain the difference between these two sausages?

– *Comment ça se prépare ?*
How do you cook it?

– *Ils viennent de quel pays ?*
Where are they from?

– *Est-ce que vous aurez des avocats demain ?*
Will you have any avocados tomorrow?

🐦 **LEARN MORE**

You can find more examples of buying food by weight in *Une charcuterie traiteur*, p.59.

For more examples of asking for explanations, you can refer to *Une pâtisserie chocolaterie*, p.45.

Le marché

Most famous

The oldest market in Paris is Le petit marché des Enfants-Rouges, rue de Bretagne. In 1777, it replaced an orphanage where the children were always dressed in red, hence its name.

Other famous markets in France include the Marché aux fleurs in Nice. It is a very colourful market that takes place every morning on the cours Saleya. Le marché des halles in Sète is a covered market famous for its fish stalls, while Le marché au gras de Samatan, which takes place every Monday, is a well-known market for *foie gras*.

Another historic market is Le marché de Louhans. Dating from the 13th century, it specialises in selling the famed poultry from the Bresse area.

And, of course, there are the famous marchés de Noël, of which those of Strasbourg and Colmar are particularly spectacular.

Quiz

Circle the words that don't belong.

A. *des endives, des carottes, des pommes, des champignons*

B. *un kilo, une livre, une gramme, une tranche*

C. *une barquette, une truffe, un cageot, un plateau*

D. *un panier, un caddie, un étalage, un cabas*

E. *les cerises, les fringues, les saucissons, les salades*

F. *un forain, un placier, un producteur, un directeur*

Answers: A. pommes, B. une tranche, C. une truffe, D. un étalage, E. les fringues, F. un directeur

KEY POINTS

Les marchés...

- are usually only open in the morning.
- are social occasions.
- vary in size depending on the time of year.
- have a mixture of small local producers and stallholders selling a large variety of produce.
- have products that are specific to a region or time of year.

Un caveau

WHAT TO EXPECT

Wine is part of France's identity and cultural heritage. Tradition, a rich wine vocabulary and great pride in the quality of French wines have made wine a part of everyday life in France.

French people have strong feelings about the wines they like and about which wine should accompany a particular food. Great attention is paid to selection, and if you listen closely as you eat in a French restaurant, you will hear knowledgeable comments about the wine served.

If you want to buy wine, larger supermarkets have a good selection, particularly in the autumn around grape-harvesting time, when many stores hold a *foire aux vins* with special offers and sampling of wines. However, if you need advice or want to discover different wines, you should go to a specialist wine merchant, a *caviste*. He will have a large range of wines on sale and will be able to help you by recommending wines that suit your tastes. Not surprisingly perhaps, nearly all of the wines will be French.

CULTURAL TIPS

When wine tasting, you should start with a white wine first, then a rosé and finally a red wine. You can, of course, skip some and start with red wine straightaway if that is what you prefer. The winegrower or wine merchant will usually serve the wines in an order that makes it easier for your palate to distinguish between them.

Many larger or well-known vineyards are accustomed to welcoming a lot of visitors. Visits may include a slideshow or a film that explains how the wine is produced, a display of photos and objects related to the vineyards, a visit to the wine store and finally a wine tasting. You will be able to purchase any wines you enjoyed and usually other regional products, too.

Un caveau

If you want to try several wines but will be driving, or you simply don't want to drink too much, you can spit the wine out into the receptacle provided, a *crachoir*, or simply empty the rest of your glass into the *crachoir* once you have sampled a wine.

Visits to vineyards are usually free, but sometimes, especially when the wine tasting includes vintage wines, there may be a small charge. This may involve the purchase of a wineglass for the tasting. The glass will be marked with the name of the estate and you can keep it as a souvenir.

Most town centres will have one or more *cavistes* with wines from all over France. These shops will be part of a national chain or owned by individuals with a passion for wine. However, in the key towns of important wine-growing areas, such as Burgundy, Alsace or the Bordeaux region, there will be several wine merchants situated near each other. These *cavistes* specialise in the wines of their region. They will have considerable knowledge of the surrounding vineyards and individual wines and can recommend wines for a particular budget or to accompany a particular dish.

IF THERE IS ONE THING THE FRENCH ARE PASSIONATE ABOUT, IT IS THEIR WINE.

◀)) KEYWORDS

un verre de vin	glass of wine
un verre à vin	wineglass
une bouteille	bottle
une dégustation	wine tasting
un vin rouge/blanc/rosé	red, white, rosé wine
un vin mousseux	sparkling wine
un vin doux	sweet wine
un vin cuit	fortified wine
un grand cru	vintage wine
le millésime	year, vintage
le marc	marc (brandy)
le bouquet	nose
la robe	colour
un mélange	blend
la grappe de raisin	bunch of grapes
le cépage	(type of) vine
le terroir	soil
le chai	wine store (house)
le bouchon	cork
déboucher	to uncork
cracher	to spit
déguster	to taste

Un caveau

If you have time and want to enjoy the complete French wine experience, you can also visit individual vineyards. Here you can discover the history of particular wines and the passion of France's winegrowers. Some of these estates have been in the same family for many generations and sometimes many centuries. You can visit the cellars and learn about winegrowing and increase your knowledge of different French wines. The importance of *terroir*, or the local soil, will be explained, and also the particular types of vine cultivated, *le cépage*.

Each estate will have its traditions. Some wines are matured in oak barrels following centuries-old customs. On some estates, bottles of sparkling wines are turned by hand regularly following a method used for champagne, *la méthode champenoise*. Some winegrowers still harvest by hand; others are experimenting with vines planted in sand. Many now talk about *une agriculture raisonnée* with fewer chemical treatments of the vines while a few are moving to totally organic production, *les vins bio*. Everywhere you go you will meet people totally involved with their work, because if there is one thing the French are passionate about, it is their wine.

🔊 IDIOMS

– *Mettre de l'eau dans son vin* means to make concessions.
– *Cuver son vin* means to sleep it off.
– *Quand le vin est tiré, il faut le boire* means there's no turning back.
– *Être entre deux vins* means to be tipsy.

Un caveau

HISTORY AND TRADITIONS

There are numerous traditions linked to wine in most regions of France. Some of the most fascinating concern the harvesting of the grapes. As the grape harvest begins, seasonal workers arrive to help. Soon the vineyards are full of lines of people moving forward gradually through the vines as they pick the grapes. Tractors pulling trailers filled to overflowing with grapes travel to and fro along the local roads. When the harvesting is finished, there is much celebration with dancing and music in the surrounding villages.

L'arrivée of the Beaujolais nouveau on the third Thursday in November is also a time of celebration. Restaurants and *cavistes* will give this young wine a prominent place, and its arrival is now an event in many other countries, too.

CULTURAL TIPS

In the famous wine-growing regions of France, there will usually be a *route des vins*. This is a specially signposted road taking you through the vineyards with suggestions for visits. In large wine-growing areas, such as the Bordeaux region, it helps to identify the different estates and the different wines that make up the general category of Bordeaux wines.

When purchasing wines, you can ask how long the wine should be stored in a wine cellar. Some wines need to be drunk within a few years or even within a year or so. Other wines, particularly *les grands crus*, the great vintage wines, will keep for many years, some for 20 or more, and improve with keeping. Indeed, wines such as these should not be drunk too soon as they need to mature. They are often referred to as *les vins de garde*, that is wines you can keep.

If you are invited to *un vin d'honneur*, this will be a reception to celebrate something, often a wedding. After the ceremony, friends and acquaintances will be invited for a glass of wine, an occasion when they can congratulate the couple. An invitation to *un vin d'honneur* does not mean you are invited to the wedding meal.

USEFUL PHRASES

— *C'est possible de déguster ?*
   Is it possible to sample the wine?
— *Je voudrais déguster ce vin blanc, s'il vous plaît.*
   I would like to try this white wine, please.
— *Je pourrais essayer le rouge, s'il vous plaît ?*
   Can I try the red, please?
— *Je préfère ce vin-là.*
   I prefer this wine.
— *Ce vin ne me plaît pas.*
   I don't like this wine.
— *C'est quel cépage ?*
   What type of vine is it?
— *Il a du bouquet.*
   It has a good nose.
— *Il est de quelle année ?*
   What year is it?
— *Il a une joli robe.*
   It's a good colour.
— *J'aime beaucoup ce vin rouge.*
   I really like this red wine.

Un caveau

La percée du vin jaune is celebrated in February. The grapes of this very distinctive wine of the Jura region are harvested late, in the second half of October. The wine is matured for a minimum of six years in oak barrels and the festival is timed to coincide with the bottling of the wine.

Traditionally, wines in France are classified as *les vins de table*, wines not linked to a particular region, *les vins de pays*, wines from a particular area made from specific types of vine, *les vins délimités de qualité supérieure* or VDQS, strictly controlled wines from a specified limited area and *les vins d'appellation contrôlée* or AOC, superior wines that are very closely monitored. However, these classifications, introduced in the 1940s, are currently being modified in line with European norms.

 *Remember*

The French produce many of the greatest wines in the world. There are, however, some very ordinary French wines. When a wine is unexceptional but drinkable, the French will call it *un vin de table*. *Le pinard* is a general term for poor wine and *la piquette* is a really poor wine.

Couper son vin sounds a strange thing to do. It literally means to cut one's wine. However, on a very warm day, or while working, that is what some French people will do. It simply means to add water, although never to a good wine.

If somebody mentions a *pot-de-vin*, they are not referring to a carafe of wine but to a bribe.

YOU WILL HEAR

– *Vous voulez déguster ?*
Would you like to sample the wine?
– *On va commencer avec ce vin blanc.*
We'll start with this white wine.
– *Vous voudriez essayer un vin rouge ?*
Do you want to try a red wine?
– *Qu'est-ce que vous en pensez ?*
What do you think of it?
– *C'est un vin de 2009.*
It's a 2009 wine.
– *C'est un vin qui est encore jeune.*
It's a wine that is still young.
– *C'est neuf euros cinquante la bouteille.*
It's nine euros fifty a bottle.
– *Vous voulez combien de bouteilles ?*
How many bottles would you like?

Un caveau

 LANGUAGE TIPS

The French have many words for being drunk. A person will be *ivre*, *soûl* or *gris* if they have drunk too much. However, if you hear that somebody was *paf*, that means they were very drunk or plastered.

Often when referring to somebody who drinks a lot, the French will make a gesture rather than use a word. This will be either a closed fist making a rotating gesture in front of the nose or the fist with a thumb pointing to the mouth and moving back and forth with the head thrown backward.

If you want to refuse a drink politely, you can simply say, *merci*, and put a hand just above your glass.

 ADVANCED USEFUL PHRASES

— *Vous pouvez me parler un peu de ce vin ?*
Can you tell me a bit about this wine?
— *Est-ce que vous avez des bouteilles dans des coffrets de présentation ?*
Do you have any bottles in presentation boxes?
— *Est-ce que ce vin est vieilli en fût de chêne ?*
Is this wine matured in oak casks?
— *Vous êtes viticulteur depuis combien de générations ?*
For how many generations have you been winegrowers?
— *Le domaine appartient à votre famille depuis longtemps ?*
Has your family owned the estate for a long time?
— *J'aime bien les vins très tanniques. Qu'est-ce que vous pouvez me recommander ?*
I like very tannic wines. What would you recommend?
— *Est-ce que vous avez un marc que nous pourrions essayer ?*
Do you have a marc brandy that we could try?
— *Si je prends 12 bouteilles, ça me fait un prix total de combien ?*
If I buy 12 bottles, what would the total price be?

 LEARN MORE

You can find other examples of asking about someone's background in *Les spécialités régionales*, p.82.

Other ways of asking for advice on a product can be found in *Le marché*, p.68.

Most famous

There are many famous wine estates in every wine-growing region of France. Not all of them allow visits, but the local tourist office can provide information on those that do.

You can also visit the *caves cooperatives* in regions where there is a lot of wine produced. These are cooperatives that market and sell the wines of several local vineyards. Many have shops that offer wine tasting and sell directly to the general public.

Le Hameau du Vin in the Beaujolais region is the achievement of a wine merchant, Georges Dubœuf, who took over a 19th century railway station and turned it into a theme park dedicated to wine. A museum, 3-D films, a wine tasting area, a shop and a restaurant are just part of the experience in this spectacular setting. The site has become a major tourist attraction.

Quiz

Fill in the blanks using the word bank below.
servir, vieillir, donner, visiter, déguster, garder

A. J'aimerais _____ ce vin rouge en premier, s'il vous plaît.

B. Je peux _____ ce vin quelques années ?

C. Quel vin vous me conseillez de _____ avec un canard à l'orange ?

D. Vous pouvez me _____ un coffret de présentation, s'il vous plaît ?

E. Combien d'années vous faites _____ ces vins-là en fûts ?

F. Est-ce que c'est possible de _____ le domaine ?

Answers: A. déguster, B. garder, C. servir, D. donner, E. vieillir, F. visiter

KEY POINTS

Cavistes and *viticulteurs*...

- will let you sample wines.
- can help you choose by giving information about their wines.
- will advise on which wines to serve with different dishes.
- will explain the wine-making process.
- may allow you to visit their estates.

Les spécialités régionales

WHAT TO EXPECT

Do you know what a *santon* **is?** Or the origin of the traditional French *béret*? Or the link between soap and Marseille? Or the story behind the striped sweaters so many French people wear? Or what happens to all the lavender grown in Provence? When you are touring France and looking for gifts or souvenirs, you will also enjoy discovering the history behind the many crafts and specialities of each region.

CULTURAL TIPS

When buying an example of a regional and traditional craft, *l'office du tourisme*, the local tourist office, can give you the names and locations of authentic manufacturers or craftsmen.

French people often wear the traditional striped sweater around their shoulders with the sleeves knotted in front, although recently this practice has become associated with a style linked to right-wing voters and is therefore shunned by some.

Men in rural areas still commonly wear the *béret basque*. If you visit a local market, you will certainly be able to spot some *béret* wearers. For women, *bérets* have become a chic accessory. They exist in many colours and are worn open rather than flat like the traditional *béret*.

LE SAVON DE MARSEILLE COMES IN A VARIETY OF COLOURS AND PERFUMES AND IS PRESENT IN GIFT SHOPS ACROSS FRANCE.

Many sites selling traditional crafts and products have workshops where you can follow the different stages of production. Some have small museums recounting the history and displaying the tools of the trade. If you want to speak with craftsmen as you visit, you will find that communication is made easier by the fact that you can see the objects they are making and observe their techniques as they explain. It's the ideal opportunity to learn more and practise your French.

Les spécialités régionales

Traditional crafts are often linked to the geography and climate of a region. The arid soil and sunshine of Provence is ideal for growing lavender. The tree-covered slopes of the Jura provide the wood for the local toy-making industry. Kaolin, a clay found in the Limoges area, is the raw material needed for its world famous porcelain.

Sometimes, a traditional way of life has led to the flowering of a local craft. In the village of Saint-James in Normandy, the Legallais family used to spin and dye the local wool and sell it, first as balls of wool and then as woollen undergarments. Local fishermen adopted the long woollen shirts as a sort of uniform because, knitted tightly and close fitting, they were reputed to be almost waterproof. Gradually, they became the distinctive blue and white striped sweaters worn by sailors and later a national fashion.

🔊 KEYWORDS

un cadeau	present
un souvenir	souvenir
un savoir-faire	know-how, expertise
l'artisanat	craft industry
un métier	trade, craft
un atelier	workshop
la fabrication	manufacture, making
fait à la main	handmade
le dessin	design, pattern
le savon	soap
la soie	silk
le bois	wood
le verre	glass
le prix	price
l'emballage	packaging
dessiner	to draw
essayer	to try on
offrir	to give
envoyer	to send
commander	to order

Les spécialités régionales

A village or even a whole town are sometimes dependent on a local craft or industry. Visit the small village of Biot in the south of France and you will be surprised at how many expert glass blowers there are. Over the centuries, the town of Limoges has become synonymous with porcelain. *Bistanclaque*, the noise made by the looms of Lyon's silkweavers, is now only a distant memory, but at one time, the sound could be heard from morning to night throughout the silk weavers' quarter of the Croix-Rousse.

Other traditional products have taken on a new life. The traditional green tablet of *le savon de Marseille*, long considered a purely utilitarian soap, now comes in a variety of colours and perfumes and is present in gift shops across France.

It's well worth taking time when visiting any region of France to discover the history and tradition behind the local speciality. As you give your gift you will also have a great story to tell.

CULTURAL TIPS

If you are looking for a gift for children, consider a Provençal *santon*. These terracotta figures, dressed in the traditional clothes of the tradespeople in a Provençal village, are amusing and colourful and you can choose between lots of different characters.

Lavender had become very old-fashioned and reduced to sachets placed in *les armoires à linge*, wardrobes where the linen was kept. Nowadays lavender essence, *l'huile essentielle de lavande,* together with diffusers and aromatherapy, has made it popular again, and of course, it is still used in perfume. When visiting a market in Provence, don't miss the opportunity to pick up a bunch of dried lavender to take both the colour and scent of Provence home with you.

Some regional products are linked to the seasons. If you want to see, for example, the harvesting and distillation of lavender, you can only do so in summer. Other sites allowing visits may only be open during the week or at certain times of the day, so it is important to check before going.

THE TREE-COVERED SLOPES OF THE JURA PROVIDE THE WOOD FOR THE LOCAL TOY-MAKING INDUSTRY.

Les spécialités régionales

HISTORY AND TRADITIONS

In early December, in households in Provence, families set up a nativity scene peopled with the traditional *santons*, or little saints. As well as the shepherds and the Wise Men, there will be Provençal characters bearing presents. These colourful terracotta figures represent traditional tradesmen, each with the tools or clothes of their trade. The tradition started after the closure of the churches during the French Revolution when families in Provence, who could no longer attend Midnight Mass, started to create nativity scenes in their own homes. Later, a market where *santons* could be purchased in November and December was established in Marseille. It still exists today.

🔊 IDIOMS

– A *cadeau*, a present, doesn't always have positive associations in French.
– *C'est pas un cadeau* means something is a real pain!
– *Ils ne font pas de cadeaux* means they don't let you off lightly.
– *Je vous fais cadeau des détails* means I'll spare you the details.
– *C'était un cadeau empoisonné* means it was more of a curse than a blessing.

🔊 USEFUL PHRASES

– *C'est typique de la région ?*
   Is it typical of this region?
– *C'est une fabrication traditionnelle ?*
   Is it made in a traditional manner?
– *C'est possible de visiter l'atelier de fabrication ?*
   Is it possible to visit the workshop?
– *Tout est fait à la main ?*
   Is everything handmade?
– *En quoi c'est fait ?*
   What's it made of?
– *Est-ce que je peux l'essayer, s'il vous plaît ?*
   Can I try it on, please?
– *Je regarde simplement, merci.*
   I'm just looking, thank you.
– *C'est trop cher pour moi.*
   It's too expensive for me.
– *C'est possible de commander en ligne ?*
   Can I order online?
– *J'en prends un de chaque, s'il vous plaît.*
   I'll take one of each, please.

Les spécialités régionales

CULTURAL TIPS

When asking questions in a craft workshop, don't forget to greet the person first by saying *bonjour*. If someone spends some time explaining things to you, you should shake their hand as you leave.

Before taking any photos, you need to check whether this is possible. Some techniques or particular patterns and designs may be patented or well-guarded secrets. Also the laws in France concerning photos of people or even famous sites are very strict, so it's always better to ask first.

Many regional products are based on long traditions. Lyon became a centre of silk making in the early 16th century and later produced many of the rich materials used in the furnishings of Versailles. The traditional *béret basque* was first used by shepherds in the 17th century to protect them from the rain. The black *béret*, like the *baguette*, became one of the symbols of France. *Le savon de Marseille* dates back even further to the 12th century. In 1688, the *Edit de Colbert* limited the use of the name to soaps produced from olive oil in the Marseille region. Its popularity resulted in *le savon de Marseille* becoming a common noun.

Sometimes nature gave a helping hand. The quality of the kaolin near Limoges gave the clay its whiteness, which contributed to the fame of Limoges porcelain, just as the fields of lavender in Provence provided the essential oils that supplied the perfume manufacturers of Grasse.

🔊 YOU WILL HEAR

— *Je peux vous renseigner ?*
   Can I help you?
— *Vous cherchez quelque chose en particulier ?*
   Are you looking for something in particular?
— *Vous connaissez nos produits ?*
   Are you familiar with our products?
— *N'hésitez pas à me demander si vous avez besoin de renseignements.*
   Don't hesitate to ask if you need further information.
— *C'est fait à la main suivant les méthodes traditionnelles.*
   It's handmade using traditional techniques.
— *Vous pouvez visiter l'atelier de fabrication si vous le souhaitez.*
   You can visit the workshop if you wish.
— *Vous prenez ceci ? Vous faites un bon choix.*
   You would like this one? You've made a good choice.
— *Vous aimeriez voir autre chose ?*
   Is there anything else you would like?

Les spécialités régionales

🔊 LANGUAGE TIPS

If you ask a question and are unable to understand the reply, you can ask the person to speak more slowly or to repeat the information:
– *Vous pouvez parler un peu plus lentement, s'il vous plaît ?*
Can you speak more slowly, please?
– *Je suis désolé, je n'ai pas compris. Vous pouvez répéter, s'il vous plaît ?*
I'm sorry, I didn't understand. Could you repeat that, please?

If you want to ask questions but find this difficult, remember that in French you can use intonation to transform a statement into a question. You simply need to make your voice go up at the end of the sentence.
– *Vous fabriquez beaucoup de santons différents ?*
Do you produce many different sorts of santons?

🔊 *Remember*

When you are buying something as a present in France, you can always ask for it to be giftwrapped. You can request this by saying:
– *Vous pouvez me faire un paquet-cadeau, s'il vous plaît ?*

Sometimes, the sales assistant will ask whether you want something giftwrapped by asking:
– *C'est pour offrir ?*

If you don't want it giftwrapped, you can simply say:
– *Non, merci. C'est pour moi.*

If you want to remind the sales assistant to remove the price, you can say:
– *Vous pouvez enlever le prix, s'il vous plaît ?*

🔊 ADVANCED USEFUL PHRASES

– *Vous pouvez m'expliquer comment c'est fait ?*
Can you explain how it's made?
– *La récolte se fait à quelle époque ?*
When is the harvest?
– *Quel dessin est le plus traditionnel ?*
Which design is the most traditional?
– *Depuis combien de temps faites-vous ce métier ?*
How long have you been doing this?
– *Est-ce que la formation est très longue ?*
Is the training period very long?
– *Il faut combien de temps pour faire un santon ?*
How long does it take to make one santon?
– *Vous avez autre chose un peu moins cher ?*
Do you have anything less expensive?
– *Est-ce que vous pouvez envoyer à l'étranger ?*
Can you ship overseas?

 **LEARN MORE**

Further examples of asking for more information about something can be found in *Le marché*, p.68.

Other ways of asking about somebody's work can be found in *Un caveau*, p.75.

Les spécialités régionales

Most famous

There are more than a hundred workshops producing *santons* in Provence. One of the oldest companies is Santons Marcel Carbonel, where *santons* have been handmade and hand-painted since 1935.

Most of the silk workshops in Lyon have closed but the Maison des Canuts in the old silk workers' quarter is well worth a visit as you can watch the Jacquard looms functioning. L'Atelier de Soierie also has a workshop and a large choice of silk products on sale.

Armor-Lux and Saint-James are two well-known names in the production of the famous *pull marin de Bretagne*. Both firms have existed for many years and their shops can be found throughout France.

Bubble glass can be found at La Verrerie de Biot, where the technique of trapping bubbles between two layers of glass was first mastered. There are several glassblowers in the village of Biot, which is a popular tourist site.

The manufacturer Bernardaud started producing high-quality porcelain in 1863. In 1986, it acquired L'Ancienne Manufacture Royale, dating back to the reign of Louis XVI. Guided visits are an opportunity to see how porcelain is made. Haviland and Royal Limoges are also famous manufacturers and there is a fascinating porcelain museum in Limoges, which is well worth a visit.

Quiz

Match the first half of the sentence with its second half.

A. *Je peux prendre...*
B. *Vous pouvez me faire...*
C. *Je peux...*
D. *C'est un dessin...*
E. *Vous avez quelque chose...*
F. *Nous pouvons visiter...*

1. *traditionnel ?*
2. *de moins cher ?*
3. *un paquet-cadeau ?*
4. *trois savons, s'il vous plaît ?*
5. *l'atelier ?*
6. *commander sur votre site ?*

Answers: A4, B3, C6, D1, E2, F5.

KEY POINTS

Les spécialités régionales...

- make good gifts or souvenirs.
- are products of traditional French craftsmanship.
- are often associated with interesting visits to workshops.
- help you understand the history and the way of life in France's different regions.
- are a way of making contact and talking with French people.

Le shopping à Paris

WHAT TO EXPECT

One of the great things about shopping in Paris is that you will have the opportunity to visit top tourist sites at the same time. Go into the famous Parisian department stores and you will also see magnificent historic buildings. Wander around le Marais quarter looking at the designer shops and you will discover one of Paris's most fascinating districts. Les Champs-Élysées may be home to the flagships of some of France's great brands, but it is also among the most famous avenues in the world.

Paris offers multiple possibilities, whether you are looking for gifts and souvenirs or just indulging in a bit of window-shopping, what the French evocatively call *faire du lèche-vitrines*, literally licking the shop windows.

Not to be missed are the big department stores. Les Galeries Lafayette and Le Printemps are next to each other in Paris's 9th *arrondissement*. Each has a long history and occupies an impressive building. Both have shops in other big cities in France, but the Paris shops are by far the most spectacular. The displays of French perfumes and beauty products alone attract huge numbers of tourists.

CULTURAL TIPS

When you are buying goods in France, the price on the item will be the amount you pay at the cash desk. Taxes are already included. Many shops also show the price in French francs as well as the price in euros. This was to help people see the equivalent price in francs when the euro was introduced but the habit has persisted, although the French franc is no longer legal tender.

The big department stores, *les grands magasins,* are famous for their window displays, particularly in December when there are elaborate themed and animated scenes that children enjoy. About 10 million people come to see these displays.

Le shopping à Paris

So many foreign tourists visit the big department stores in Paris that sales assistants who speak other languages, including Mandarin, are employed, especially for the perfume and beauty products departments.

Sales, *les soldes*, are strictly regulated in France. There are two main periods, each lasting five weeks: one in mid-January and the other in late June. Sales always start on a Wednesday. Recently, additional sales periods have been allowed. The dates can be freely chosen, but they must not exceed one period of two weeks or two periods of one week per year.

During the sales, you will see a succession of different signs in shop windows. When you see *deuxième démarque*, usually about two weeks after the start of the sales, this means there is a second markdown. Sometimes this is shown as *nouvelle démarque*. A *remise* together with a given percentage is also a reduction. Finally, towards the end of the period, you may also see *dernière démarque*, final markdown.

Le Marais is a very different experience. It is a fascinating district of narrow streets and squares situated on the right bank of the Seine. The place des Vosges is its focal point with its arcades and restaurants and, tucked in a corner, the house of the celebrated French author, Victor Hugo. The quarter's beautiful old town houses, some of which date back to the 17th century, house art galleries and museums. As you wander through the streets full of clothing and jewellery boutiques, don't forget to peek into the courtyards — many young fashion designers have moved into the picturesque 18-century workshops that surround them.

PARIS OFFERS MULTIPLE POSSIBILITIES, WHETHER YOU ARE LOOKING FOR GIFTS AND SOUVENIRS OR JUST INDULGING IN A BIT OF WINDOW-SHOPPING.

 IDIOMS

– *Acheter chat en poche* means to buy a pig in a poke.
– *Une grosse pointure* is a bigwig.
– *Vider son sac* means to get it off one's chest.
– *Je les mets tous dans le même sac* means they are as bad as each other.

Le shopping à Paris

The long rue du Faubourg-Saint-Honoré is the street to explore if you are looking for luxury goods or antiques. Again you can mix tourism and history as you shop, for the street is also famous for l'Élysée, the official residence of the French president, numerous embassies and some of the capital's luxury hotels.

Other shopping experiences you will not want to miss are Paris's covered galleries, the famous shops near La Madeleine, the boutiques of Saint-Germain-des-Prés and for chains, the rue de Rivoli. The famous historic flea market, les Puces de Saint-Ouen, is also well worth a visit.

No shopping agenda in Paris is complete without a trip to Les Champs-Élyées though. Whether you walk down this celebrated and always bustling avenue in the daytime, or at night with all the lights, it is a special experience. You may well want to buy something here just to say that you bought it on Les Champs-Élysées. Yet again you will find that *le shopping* in Paris takes you to the heart of the capital's history and identity.

◄)) KEYWORDS

les grands magasins	department store
le rayon	department
le rez-de-chaussée	ground floor, first floor (US)
le premier étage	first floor, second floor (US)
le sous-sol	basement
les produits de beauté	beauty products
la maroquinerie	leather goods
les vêtements hommes/ femmes/enfants	men's/women's/children's clothing
une cabine d'essayage	fitting room
la taille	size
la pointure	shoe size
la couleur	colour
une vendeuse	sales assistant
la caisse	cash desk
un foulard	scarf
un sac à main	handbag
du parfum	perfume
un pull	sweater, pullover
une cravate	tie
un collier	necklace
des boucles d'oreille	earrings
un portefeuille	wallet

Le shopping à Paris

HISTORY AND TRADITIONS

Large department stores were first seen in Europe's main cities in the 19th century. The Industrial Revolution meant that garments could be produced at a lower unit cost and the growing middle class had money to spend.

La Samaritaine was the largest store in the French capital. Situated on the banks of the Seine, it opened in 1869. It grew rapidly as its owner acquired the surrounding shops. From its rooftop terrace there was a magnificent view over the city and the store was much-loved by Parisians. La Samaritaine was closed in 2005. In new plans for the site, it will no longer exist as one large store.

CULTURAL TIPS

Exchanging goods in France is not always easy. You can usually exchange faulty goods without difficulty if you have proof of purchase, but you cannot always exchange something because you have simply changed your mind. Sometimes stores will give you a credit but will not refund your purchase. Goods bought during sales cannot usually be exchanged.

Department stores in Paris remain open late one day a week, usually a Thursday, when they close at nine or ten o'clock in the evening. They are not open on Sundays except in the run-up to Christmas. Many shops on Les Champs-Élysées remain open until midnight and are open on Sundays.

🔊 USEFUL PHRASES

— *Je regarde seulement, merci.*
I'm just looking, thank you.
— *Où est le rayon maroquinerie, s'il vous plaît ?*
Where is the leather goods department, please?
— *Je cherche un foulard en soie pour une amie.*
I'm looking for a silk scarf for a friend.
— *Je peux essayer ce pull ?*
Can I try this sweater, please?
— *Vous l'avez dans une autre couleur ?*
Do you have it in another colour?
— *Désolée mais ça ne me va pas.*
I'm sorry, but it doesn't suit me.
— *Quel est le prix, s'il vous plaît ?*
What's the price, please?
— *C'est en cuir ?*
Is it made of leather?
— *Je le prends.*
I'll take it.
— *Où est-ce qu'on paie ?*
Where do I pay?

NOT TO BE MISSED

Le shopping à Paris

IN PARIS YOU WILL HAVE THE OPPORTUNITY TO VISIT TOP TOURIST SITES WHILE YOU SHOP.

Le Printemps was innovative in its architecture. The use of visible ironwork, the addition of a central staircase and distinctive lighting together with the introduction of lifts helped it to prosper and draw customers. It was the first store to introduce annual sales, and its giant window displays with specially designed dressmakers' mannequins soon became an attraction, too.

Les Galeries Lafayette is also an impressive building. Opened in 1908 and officially inaugurated in 1912, it has a magnificent interior with a glass dome. Together with Le Printemps, it has made the boulevard Haussmann one of the grandest and most visited shopping areas in the world.

The Le Marais quarter used to be marshland, hence its name. However, from the 12th century on, it was populated by religious orders. Later, in the 17th century, many French nobles built residences there. But after the Revolution, the nobles gone, tradesmen built their workshops in the courtyards. The quarter is now protected to preserve its distinctive character.

🔊 *Remember*

When you are inquiring on which floor a particular department is, the French do not count the ground floor or street level, *le rez-de-chaussée*. The floor above this level is the first floor, *le premier étage*; for Americans it would be the second floor.

When you walk through the beauty department, a shop assistant may ask you:
– *Je vous parfume ?*

If you agree, they will spray you with perfume. Sometimes this will be a perfume they are promoting; sometimes you will be able to choose a perfume. There is no obligation to purchase.

When paying at the cash desk, you may be asked if you have a loyalty card:
– *Vous avez la carte du magasin ?*
– *Vous avez la carte de fidélité ?*

🔊 YOU WILL HEAR

– *Je peux vous aider ?*
Can I help you?
– *Le rayon chaussures est au troisième étage.*
The shoe department is on the third floor.
– *Qu'est-ce que vous cherchez comme sac ?*
What sort of bag are you looking for?
– *Vous voulez l'essayer ?*
Do you want to try it on?
– *Vous voulez voir d'autres modèles ?*
Do you want to see some other designs?
– *Vous préférez la cravate bleue ou la verte ?*
Do you prefer the blue tie or the green one?
– *C'est en argent, madame.*
It's made of silver, madam.
– *La caisse est juste là-bas.*
The cash desk is just over there.

Eating and shopping in France   93

Le shopping à Paris

Most famous

Paris's celebrated department store, Le Printemps, opened in 1865, and Les Galeries Lafayette opened in 1908. Both are situated on the prestigious boulevard Haussmann. The two stores total more than 120 million visitors a year.

L'avenue des Champs-Élysées is one of the most beautiful avenues in the world. The 70-metre wide avenue links la place de la Concorde to la place Charles-de-Gaulle where l'Arc de Triomphe de l'Étoile stands in the centre. Along the avenue are the shops of many of the world's great brands. The shops on the even-number side of the avenue have the most visitors because it is the sunniest side.

The avenue is also the setting for the great military parade on Bastille Day, the 14th of July, and also the final stage of the Tour de France bicycle race. The traditional illuminations are switched on at the end of November and, on New Year's Eve, traffic is barred so that everyone can celebrate freely on Les Champs-Élysées.

 LANGUAGE TIPS

When you know what you are looking for, whether it be a scarf or a handbag or a tie, make sure you know the French word for it before going into the shop. Then you can simply say:
– *Je cherche un foulard en soie.*

This allows you to concentrate on the information you receive from the sales assistant. If you have any particular requirements, such as a traditional design, you can specify this, too:
– *Je cherche un foulard en soie avec un dessin traditionnel.*

The more information you can give, the less you will have to cope with answering questions in French and the more you will be able to take the initiative and control the conversation.

 LEARN MORE

You can find other examples of asking for advice in *Un caveau*, p.75.

For other examples of asking for more information, you can refer to *Un restaurant*, p.22.

Le shopping à Paris

🔊 ADVANCED USEFUL PHRASES

– *Les vêtements femmes sont à quel étage, s'il vous plaît ?*
Women's clothes are on which floor, please?

– *Je vais réfléchir, mais merci pour votre aide.*
I'm going to think about it, but thank you for your help.

– *J'ai besoin de quelques renseignements, s'il vous plaît.*
I need some information, please.

– *Je peux vous demander conseil ?*
Can I ask your advice?

– *Vous pouvez m'aider à choisir un parfum, s'il vous plaît ?*
Could you help me choose a perfume, please?

– *Vous avez des chemises à manches courtes, s'il vous plaît ?*
Do you have short-sleeved shirts, please?

– *Avez-vous le même en plus petit ?*
Do you have this in a smaller size?

– *Je cherche un sac à main en cuir mais celui-ci est trop grand.*
I'm looking for a leather handbag, but this one is too big.

Put the following dialogue in the correct order.

A. *Une taille moyenne, s'il vous plaît.*

B. *Je préfère le bleu, s'il vous plaît.*

C. *Merci.*

D. *Vous voulez l'essayer ?*

E. *Bonjour, je cherche un pull marin.*

F. *Oui, je l'aime bien. Je vais le prendre.*

G. *Oui, je préfère.*

H. *Ah, ça vous va très bien.*

I. *Voilà, j'en ai un en bleu et un en rouge.*

J. *La cabine d'essayage est juste ici.*

K. *Oui, il vous faut quelle taille ?*

Answers: E, K, A, I, B, D, G, J, C, H, F.

KEY POINTS

Le shopping à Paris...

- Paris's big department stores are in historic buildings.
- Window displays during the end-of-year holidays are a big attraction.
- All prices include taxes.
- Department stores often stay open late on Thursdays.
- There are big sales twice a year, starting in January and late June.

As they say in French

- *« Le vin est la partie intellectuelle d'un repas. »*
  Alexandre Dumas

- *« Une journée sans vin est une journée sans soleil. »*
  Proverbe provençal

- *« Les jours sont des fruits et notre rôle est de les manger. »*
  Jean Giono

- *« C'est la capitale qui, surtout, fait les mœurs des peuples ; c'est Paris qui fait les Français. »*
  Montesquieu

- *« Une femme sans parfum est une femme sans avenir. »*
  Coco Chanel

Pam Bourgeois' name has long been associated with creative and effective language learning methods. Her techniques are based on years of experience running language schools for an international clientele and creating language-study materials in Europe and Africa. She has worked as a consultant in business French for the BBC and co-authored OBJECTIFS: ASSIGNMENTS IN PRACTICAL LANGUAGE SKILLS (Cambridge University Press).

Pam has lived and worked for over 25 years in France where she established language schools, created and was editor-in-chief of several language magazines and developed a series of over 30 audio learning guides in three languages.

Her expertise in language acquisition and passion for cultural understanding inspired her to create Kolibri Languages and publish a series of practical guides to lifestyle, manners and language. The guides highlight the importance of cultural awareness when learning a language or visiting another country.

Photo credits

p.10 top left: Kari Masson
p.15: Kari Masson
p.26: Jan Krandendok / Shutterstock.com
p.28: Keith Levit / Shutterstock.com
p.36: Cile Borders
p.37 top right: Kari Masson
p.40-41: Hilde Vanstraelen / biewoef.be
p.41 bottom right: Kari Masson
p.50 top left: Kari Masson
p.52 top right: Kari Masson
p.68-69 bottom: Kari Masson
p.70 top: Kari Masson
p.72 top left, fourth centre: Kari Masson
p.73 all centre: Kari Masson
p.90 two centre: Jan Krandendok / Shutterstock.com
p.92-93: Tupangato / Shutterstock.com
p.93 centre: Stefan Ataman / Shutterstock.com
p.95 bottom: Jan Krandendok / Shutterstock.com
Shutterstock.com

Dépôt légal : août 2012
Imprimé en France (Printed in France) juillet 2012
par Chevillon Imprimeur, 26 boulevard Kennedy, 89100 Sens